Political Entrepreneurship

Josef Lentsch

Political Entrepreneurship

How to Build Successful Centrist Political
Start-ups

Springer

Josef Lentsch
NEOS Lab
Vienna, Wien
Austria

ISBN 978-3-030-02860-2   ISBN 978-3-030-02861-9   (eBook)
https://doi.org/10.1007/978-3-030-02861-9

Library of Congress Control Number: 2018959839

Cover illustration: Nicole Heiling

This Springer imprint is published by the registered company Springer Nature Switzerland AG
The registered company address is: Gewerbestrasse 11, 6330 Cham, Switzerland

"You have read a lot about startups in business, but if you want to know how Silicon Valley style startups look in politics, read this. Its author is not only writing about political entrepreneurs, he is one of them."
—Ivan Krastev, *Chairman of the Centre for Liberal Strategies in Sofia, and permanent Fellow at the Institute of Human Sciences in Vienna*

"No one understands better what it takes to take a political start up from ideation to the parliament than Josef Lentsch. In 'Political Entrepreneurship' he combines first-hand experience with a thoughtful review of what we know about entrepreneurship in the interest of society."
—Johanna Mair, *Professor of Organization, Strategy and Leadership at the Hertie School of Governance, and Co-Director Global Innovation for Impact Lab at Stanford University*

"Josef Lentsch has produced a fascinating, commanding guide to the new, insurgent players shaking up traditional party systems and reinvigorating liberal politics. Political Entrepreneurship is essential reading for anyone who wants to understand today's fragmented and disrupted European politics—and the European politics of the future."
—Jeremy Cliffe, *Charlemagne columnist, The Economist*

"The rarest of events has occurred—a new political species has appeared in the European eco-system, the centrist political start up. From Macron's *En Marche* in France to Spain's Ciudadanos, a new type of political actor has emerged. Few are better positioned to tell this Europe-wide story than Josef Lentsch who has had a front-seat view on this important political transformation that is shaking Europe. A dramatic and important account."
—Daniel Ziblatt, *Eaton Professor of Government, Harvard University and co-author of How Democracies Die*

For my sons Jann and Piet

Preface

On 27 September 2013, I flew from London, where I and my family were living at the time, to Vienna. My 2-year-old son was sitting on my lap. His 6-month-old brother had stayed behind with my wife in London. It had been a year since the founding of NEOS, an Austrian political start-up. After a long and exhausting summer, during which I had helped mobilise Austrian voters abroad, and shuttled between London and Vienna as a Founding Board member, Election Day was approaching. It had been a frantic campaign. The polls had only picked us up in the final weeks. Would it be enough?

Two days later, I was standing in a large crowd in front of the TV in the NEOSphere, the headquarters of NEOS on the top floor of a non-descript building in Neubau, Vienna's gentrified-hip seventh district. We were all staring at the screen, anxiously waiting for the first exit poll, expected at 5 pm. We had no hope of winning. Success for us would be clearing the 4% threshold above which we would be represented in parliament.

The exit poll projection was expressed as a bar chart. The first column shot up. Then the second. Both the Social Democrats and the Conservatives had lost. In third place, the far-right Freedom Party had gained. No surprises. The Greens had won as well. Now came the other new kid in town, the populist Team Stronach. They had made it, too. Finally, our turn. The seconds seemed longer than normal. Finally, the pink column shot up and stopped just below 5%. The crowd erupted. In a split second, the tension was released in screaming, jumping, hugging and crying for joy.

A piece on the Austrian election in the *New York Times* a couple of days later said: "The new party, known as NEOS, in German short for New Austria, was the surprise of the day."

We had made history.

It took me some time to understand that we were not—not by a long shot—the only ones. That there were many other groups across Europe who had identified the same problems we had and arrived at the same conclusion:

If not us, who?
If not now, when?

* * *

Politics, I have found, is an exhilarating but often bruising team sport, played 24 h a day, 7 days a week. For politicians, it takes self-discipline to draw appropriate lines, time and again, between their private and public lives. It takes integrity to stay grounded and stick to one's values. It takes self-reflection to keep stepping out of the system and questioning whether one is still working in the spirit that led to one getting involved in politics in the first place. This *place*. Politics, NEOS co-founder Matthias Strolz likes to say, is the place where we meet to agree how we want to live well together. In this sense, it is *essential*. There is no substitute for it, apart from war, which von Clausewitz said was "the continuation of politics by other means".

I was born in 1976, in a stable Western democracy, towards the end of the Cold War. The town where I grew up was 15 min by car from the Iron Curtain. I was 13 when the Berlin Wall fell. Just a couple of months earlier, a few kilometres from my house, the foreign ministers of Austria and Hungary had jointly cut the barbed wire fence between our countries. I was 19 when Austria joined the European Union. I am part of the MTV generation. Sandwiched between Generation X and the Millennials, we were perhaps the first global generation and the last to grow up without personal computers. We were witnesses to a dramatic change in politics as well as technology at a critical stage of our lives. We knew that things could be different, that things *could* change for the better and that politics could be a force for good.

I have been Director of NEOS Lab, the think-and-do tank of NEOS, for 5 years now. It has been a wild and, at times, a bewildering ride. We entered the political arena with high hopes and an overdose of optimism. Many of us, including me, had been, or still were, entrepreneurs, bringing their hands-on, can-do attitude to the political arena. We had to learn that the political status quo can be frustratingly resilient to change and that politics is a craft that requires constant honing. The trick is to learn to work the system without becoming a part of it.

We did not always live up to our own expectations. Once your hands are dirty, what's a little more dirt gonna do? Political entrepreneurs are no saints. Some of them may be heroes (I really think so), but all are human, fallible and prone to fail.

When we stumbled, we got back on our feet. There is a Japanese proverb: "fall seven times and stand up eight". This is what entrepreneurs do. They eat failure for breakfast.

As Max Weber, himself a failed politician, proclaimed 100 years ago in his lecture on "Politics as a Vocation":

> Politics is a strong and slow boring of hard boards. It takes both passion and perspective. Certainly all historical experience confirms the truth—that man would not have attained the possible unless time and again he had reached out for the impossible. But to do that a man must be a leader, and not only a leader but a hero as well, in a very sober sense of the word. And even those who are neither leaders nor heroes must arm themselves with that steadfastness of heart that can brave even the crumbling of all hopes. This is necessary right now, or else men will not be able to attain even that which is possible today. (Weber 1919)

Promoting what today seems almost impossible politically, in the interest of progress and a better future for us all, is what the political start-ups I describe in the pages that follow were founded for.

This is not just a national struggle. Politics today is regional and global. What was previously a struggle between the Left and Right has turned into a struggle between open and closed societies and economies. Some of the most successful political entrepreneurs of late have been champions of the closed—UKIP in the UK, PiS in Poland, the PVV in the Netherlands, M5S in Italy, AfD in Germany or, across the pond, Donald Trump in the USA: "Populist, authoritarian European parties of the right or left now enjoy nearly twice as much support as they did in 2000, and are in government or in a ruling coalition in nine countries." ("The new political divide", *The Economist*, July 30, 2016.)

In the battle for openness, the centre must hold. But that is not enough. The political centre must transform itself, if it is to prevail against the populists and extremists. This is not just a question of policies; it is also a question of organisation.

Once NEOS established international contacts, I was delighted to learn that in this fight for openness and transformation, a surprising number of centrist political start-ups all over Europe and around the world, liberal, centre-left and centre-right, have emerged in recent years. And I firmly believe this is only the beginning of a much larger shift that will produce more centrist political start-ups.

History accumulates, but it does not necessarily progress. On the contrary, in many regards, liberal democracy is "in recession", as Larry Diamond wrote ("Facing up to the Democratic Recession", *Journal of Democracy*, January, 2015).

It is time to embark on a new history. I have written this book in the belief that political entrepreneurs have a key role to play in shaping it.

Vienna, Wien, Austria   Josef Lentsch
November 2018

Acknowledgements

My thanks are due to Angelika Mlinar, Matthias Strolz, Beate Meinl-Reisinger, the Board and the team of NEOS Lab and the European Liberal Forum for their support; Nicolas Stühlinger for the verbal sparring and crucial support in the early stages of the project; Johannes Glaeser and Jessica Fäcks, my editors at Springer; Veit Dengler for challenging and revising; Ivan March for proofreading; Sandra Glück-Taglieber for helping with transcripts; the Impact Hub Vienna for providing the perfect writing environment; and Tom Lloyd for helping me cross the finish line.

Many thanks also to my interview partners for allowing me learn from them:

Ciudadanos: Antonio Roldán Monés, Begoña Villacís, Carmen Cassa, Fran Hervías, Jorge San Miguel Lobeto, Jose Manuel Villegas, Melisa Rodríguez Hernández, Vicente Rodrigo.

En Marche: Aziz François Ndiaye, Grégoire Potton, Julien Tassy, Ludovic Bain, Matthieu Chauzy, Stéphane Roques.

Momentum: Andras Fekete-Györ, Katka Cseh.

NEOS: Angelika Mlinar, Beate Meinl-Reisinger, Feri Thierry, Grace Pardy, Matthias Strolz, Michael Bernhard, Michael Schiebel, Nick Donig, Stefan Egger, Veit Dengler.

Nowoczesna: Adam Szłapka, Joanna Burnos, Joanna Schmidt, Katarzyna Lubnauer, Mateusz Maciej, Miłosz Hodun, Pawel Rabiej, Ryszard Petru.

Progresívne: Ivan Stefunko, Martin Dubéci.

Yesh Atid: Yair Lapid.

Experts who generously shared their insights with me include Csaba Tóth, Guillaume Liegey, Harald Katzmair, Małgorzata Bonikowska and Ronan Harrington.

I also received invaluable inspiration, help, feedback and advice from Adam Lent, Andreas Pohancenik, Alexander Görlach, Andreas Lechner, Anthony Painter, Christoph Konrath, Dan Berwick, Dieter Feierabend, Douglas Hoyos, Edward Strasser, Ernst Piper, Ian Marquardt, Isabelle Nüssli, Johanna Mair, Jeremy Cliffe, Joseph Dengler, Konstantina Zoehrer, Lars Maydell, Luke Fuszard, Manuel Hartung, Marie Ringler, Martin Ängeby, Michael Ambjorn, Michael Cottakis, Niki Scherak, Paul Hilder and Stefan Windberger.

Finally, my wife, Alena Buyx, gave me the time I needed to write, was my most important critic, encouraged me when I questioned myself and was my role model for getting stuff done.

Introduction

I wrote the first lines of this book the day after NEOS re-entered parliament on 15 October 2017. Despite the highly polarised election battle, which saw the Greens ejected from parliament after 31 years, NEOS increased its share of the vote, compared to when it first entered in 2013. It was the first independently founded liberal party in Western Europe since 1968 to have managed that.

A few months earlier, Emmanuel Macron and La République En Marche had turned the French political system upside down. A few months later, in December 2017, Ciudadanos won the highly contested elections in Catalonia and subsequently began to poll as one of the three largest parties in Spain.

This book is the story of European centrist political start-ups like Ciudadanos, En Marche and NEOS. They not only practise a different politics, they practise politics differently. It is the story of political entrepreneurs who are re-inventing the political centre. The lessons learned are relevant not only for continental Europe, but also for the increasingly polarised politics of the UK, the USA and elsewhere.

Traditionally, political science has focused on two kinds of new political party: new left, Green and left-libertarian parties in particular and new right parties ("Studying the Electoral Success of New Political Parties: A Methodological Approach", Simon Hug, *Party Politics*, VOL 6, 2000). The political centre is seldom mentioned. But it is the Centre, and particularly the push of centrist political start-ups against the nationalists and populists, that will drive the direction of democratic transformation in the twenty-first century. It will either regress and decline, or progress and renew. This book offers some ideas on how to help liberal democracies move on.

Political start-ups are like business start-ups. There is the original act of creation and then there is the organisation's development. This book is similar: first there is a how-to guide for aspiring political entrepreneurs and then a guide for practitioners such as political executives, functionaries, advisors and consultants. If you're only interested in practical matters, you can skip the first two chapters.

The new, clearly defined and well-researched concept of political entrepreneurship presented at the beginning should be of interest to political scientists, however, and I hope the many parallels and touchpoints with social entrepreneurship will be of use to people involved in this field.

Most of the data for this book were generated by qualitative research on seven political start-ups: La Republique En Marche in France, Ciudadanos in Spain,

Momentum in Hungary, Nowoczesna in Poland, Progresívne in Slovakia, NEOS in Austria and Yesh Atid in Israel. Apart from the latter, all are European and distinctly pro-European.

The seven political start-ups I have assembled were chosen for their homogeneity (politically centrist, built from scratch, entered the national stage after 2010) and their variety. Some, such as Progresívne, have yet to contest their first national elections. Others, such as En Marche, have already entered government.

In the course of a year I conducted more than 40 semi-structured interviews with people at all levels, from chairpersons and activists to political experts. Most of the interviews were done in person, in Bratislava, Budapest, Madrid, Paris, Vienna and Warsaw. I conducted a few interviews via Skype.

I also conducted desk research into the literature in such areas as democratic decline and renewal, new political parties, political leadership and political and social entrepreneurship.

The book begins, in Chap. 1, with a practical theory of political entrepreneurship. Building on classical and newer definitions of entrepreneurship as well as social and civic entrepreneurship, it highlights similarities as well as differences between these concepts and shows political entrepreneurship to be the "third wave" of entrepreneurship.

Chapter 2, "Liberal Democracies in Crisis", offers a summary of the challenges faced by liberal democracies in Europe and around the world, as well as how politics need to change to deal with them effectively. Drawing on recent literature on the topic, it reviews the argument that for more than a decade, democracy has been "in recession". The resulting civic dissatisfaction is fertile ground for populists, but also for centrist political start-ups.

Common constraints political entrepreneurs face are analysed in Chap. 3, "Leadership". Among them are leading without power, leading under extreme uncertainty, leading without clients, leading in times of crisis and leading from the future.

Chapter 4, "Understanding Political Systems", offers insights and anecdotes of how political entrepreneurs have developed a deep understanding of the political systems around them over time. It also shows various routes to how political entrepreneurs arrive at a vision of a new politics, some more intellectual, some more action-based and some more experiential.

Chapter 5, "Building Models for Political Change", presents the beginning of a step-by-step path to building a political start-up from scratch. It highlights the required resources and individual roles, like sparring partners, mentors, accomplices or first followers.

Chapter 6, "(Co)-Design", presents the bewildering array of choices political entrepreneurs face when designing a political start-up. It provides insights into various tried and tested strategic options for the organisation design of a centrist political start-up.

"Getting competitive", Chap. 7, gives examples how political start-ups gathered momentum and built up critical mass through initiatives like petitions or roadshows. It also narrates how data and ideas gathered throughout those initiatives were systematically captured, for example by En Marche in their project "La Grande Marche".

Chapter 8, "Ready, Steady, Go", presents examples of how the portrayed political start-ups ran their campaigns, from the first to the last day. It provides practical examples of how they budgeted, how they targeted their electorate and how they arrived at the messaging. In the second part, the chapter provides insights into factors behind electoral successes and failures.

Paradoxically, entering parliament can be a traumatic experience for a political start-up. They suddenly have to manage the problem of success. Chapter 9, "Enter", presents key tasks after entering, like re-integrating, re-engaging or consolidating the political start-up.

In Chap. 10, "Growing up and Handing Over", I recount how the portrayed political start-ups scale over time, what advice experienced political entrepreneurs have for the ones who are just getting started and what challenges they currently face either in opposition or in government. In the second part, the chapter presents two examples of how political entrepreneurs dealt with handing over the leadership of their political start-up.

The final Chap. 11, "Political Entrepreneurs and the Evolution of Democracy", takes a look into the future of political entrepreneurship: what's next? Will some of the ideas be applied by political intrapreneurs in traditional parties? How will the political party of the future look like? And what is required to help centrist political start-ups win the race against their populist foes?

In the Appendix, you can find the road map to political transformation, which provides a visual summary of all stages of political entrepreneurship and respective key tasks, as presented in the book.

For the development of the road map, I drew on three primary sources: firstly, a literature review of political entrepreneurship; secondly, the framework for social entrepreneurship developed by Roger L. Martin and Sally R. Osberg in "Getting Beyond Better: how Social Entrepreneurship works" (Harvard Business Review Press, 2015). Thirdly, I have incorporated the information and insights from more than 40 interviews conducted with political entrepreneurs and experts and their feedback on the draft versions of the book.

As a reflective practitioner, I hope to provide readers with an understanding of the political start-up phenomenon, and to budding political entrepreneurs I offer ideas, tools and, most importantly, encouragement.

Go on then. Change the world.

Contents

About the Author

Josef Lentsch is Founding Director of NEOS Lab, the party academy of NEOS in Vienna, Austria. He was a founding board member of NEOS.

Prior to that, he was the International Director for The Royal Society for the Encouragement of Arts, Manufactures and Commerce in London. Before, he co-founded, managed and sold UNIPORT, Austria's largest career service for students and graduates.

He holds an MSc in Psychology from the University of Vienna and an MPA in Public Administration from Harvard University.

List of Tables

Introducing Political Entrepreneurship

1

Ivan Stefunko is a bearded, 41-year old Slovak serial entrepreneur and angel investor with a particular focus on the media and Internet spaces. He is married with three children, and studied Political Science in Banská Bytrica and Sciences Po in Paris, where he was a contemporary of Emmanuel Macron. "It's funny", Stefunko said when we talked in April 2018 via Skype. "He was my classmate. I only recognised him when Sciences Po published his picture from those days."

In November, 2017 he and other entrepreneurs founded Progresívne Slovensko (Progressive Slovakia), a progressive liberal political start-up.

"Traditionally, in central and eastern Europe, you've had two types of entrepreneur" Stefunko explained: "those who have stolen or, more euphemistically, 'privatised', businesses, and those who have inherited them. Now, there's a new generation of entrepreneurs in their early 40s or younger. They do not have the same sense of entitlement. They are socially responsible entrepreneurs, and very different from what we have seen in the last 20 or 25 years in Slovakia."

What Stefunko talks about and practises exemplify what I calls "the third wave" of entrepreneurship.

1.1 Entrepreneurship

"Entrepreneurship is the pursuit of opportunity beyond resources currently controlled", wrote Howard Stevenson of the Harvard Business School ("What is Entrepreneurship", Thomas R. Eisenmann, *Harvard Business Review*, 2013). I know of no better definition. *Inc.* magazine called it "the best answer ever" ("What's an Entrepreneur? The best answer ever", Eric Schurenberg, *Inc.*, January 9, 2012). Stevenson knew what he was talking about, in theory and practice: he is often said to have been the most successful fundraiser in the history of Harvard University.

© Springer Nature Switzerland AG 2019
J. Lentsch, *Political Entrepreneurship*,
https://doi.org/10.1007/978-3-030-02861-9_1

Entrepreneurship is thus a "quest"; a self-directed activity that does not necessarily feel like work (often the opposite), but requires a strong focus on implementing a plan and sustained commitment ("Civic Entrepreneurship", Charles Leadbeater, and Sue Goss, *Demos*, 1998).

Entrepreneurship is about trying to achieve something others regard as impossible or seeing opportunities others don't see, with a focus on solutions rather than problems. It means making the most of time- and situation-based "windows" that open and may close again soon, while recognising there are risks, as well as potential rewards.

"Beyond resources currently controlled" means entrepreneurship is about dealing creatively with constraints, leveraging limited resources, and trying to recruit others and their resources to the enterprise.

According to Joseph Schumpeter, the Austrian Harvard Professor famous for his research on entrepreneurship and the term "creative destruction", entrepreneurs innovate ("The Theory of Economic Development in the History of Economic Thought." Ludwig von Mises, Macmillan, 1968). Schumpeter identified five types of entrepreneurial, as opposed to incremental, innovation:

1. the introduction of a new good… or of a new quality of a good,
2. a new method of production,
3. the opening of a new market,
4. the conquest of a new source of supply of raw materials or half-manufactured goods,
5. the breaking up of a monopoly position.

Entrepreneurs can be found in all walks of life. As William Baumol wrote in his classic 1990 paper, "entrepreneurs are always with us and always play some substantial role. But there are a variety of roles among which the entrepreneur's efforts can be reallocated" ("Entrepreneurship: Productive, Unproductive, and Destructive", *Journal of Political Economy*). Baumol's conclusion that some of those roles are productive for society, some are unproductive, and some are positively destructive, is consistent with the types of entrepreneur Stefunko identified above.

Entrepreneurship is not an inherently morally good or bad activity. However, the US and other cultures have a long history of painting entrepreneurs either as heroes or villains. The Right has tended to glorify entrepreneurs (as in Ayn Rand's 1957 novel, "Atlas Shrugged", which served as the manifesto of Rand's libertarian philosophy of Objectivism). The Left has tended to vilify them.

1.2   Social Entrepreneurship

This right/left divide in the stance towards entrepreneurship started to dissolve in the 1980s. Organisations like the Ashoka began to relate social justice, traditionally a domain of the left, and entrepreneurship, by championing entrepreneurial solutions to social challenges. The "social entrepreneur" was born.

To Ashoka, "social entrepreneurs are individuals with innovative solutions to society's most pressing social, cultural, and environmental challenges. They are ambitious and persistent—tackling major issues and offering new ideas for systems-level change" (https://www.ashoka.org/en/focus/social-entrepreneurship).

The author and journalist David Bornstein thinks that Social Entrepreneurship is mainly about "how business and management skills can be applied to achieve social ends". As he writes in "How to Change the World: Social Entrepreneurs and the Power of New Ideas" (Oxford University Press, 2010), Ashoka, founded in 1980 by the former McKinsey consultant Bill Drayton, "began in the fashion of a venture capital firm, seeking high yields from modest, well-targeted investments. However, the returns it seeks are not in profits, but in advances in education, environmental protection, rural development, poverty alleviation, human rights, care for the disabled, care for children at risk and other fields."

Peter Drucker, the management guru, saw social entrepreneurs as people who raise the "performance capacity of society" ("Flashes of Genius", George Gendron, *Inc.*, May 15, 1996). To achieve that, social entrepreneurs often have to help build and organise this capacity in the first place.

In their book "Getting beyond better: how Social Entrepreneurship works" (op. cit.), Martin and Osberg define Social Entrepreneurship as follows:

- The identification of a stable but inherently unjust equilibrium that causes the exclusion, marginalisation or suffering of a segment of humanity...
- The development, testing, refining, and scaling of an equilibrium-shifting solution...
- The forging of a new stable equilibrium that unleashes new value for society, releases trapped potential, or alleviates suffering. In this new state, an ecosystem is created around the new equilibrium that sustains and grows it, extending the benefit across society.

These definitions of Social Entrepreneurship distinguish it from morally neutral entrepreneurship in three critical aspects. First, it is meant to achieve morally loaded, *positive* change (which, of course, does not make it less controversial). Second, it aims not just for incremental societal improvements, but for certain kinds of major social innovations that lead to comprehensive system transformations, and ultimately to new equilibria. And third, the definitions make clear that Social Entrepreneurship is inherently, if not explicitly, *political*.

Ashoka, the Impact Hub Network, Teach For All and other platforms in this space have created a global ecosystem fostering and empowering social entrepreneurs around the world. They have also succeeded in popularising the concept: a Google search for the term "Social Entrepreneurship" in May, 2018 returned more than 5.4 million hits. For comparison, "liberalism" returned 16.3 million hits, just three times more. In short, Social Entrepreneurship has become the second global wave of entrepreneurship.

1.3   Civic Entrepreneurship

"Civic entrepreneurship" is another closely related term. It is the adoption of an entrepreneurial approach to empowering civil society. In an article for *Social Europe* ("Why Europe Needs Civic Entrepreneurs", November 10, 2017) Professor Alberto Alemanno of the École des hautes études commerciales in Paris and Michael Cottakis of the London School of Economics advocate civic entrepreneurship, because: "Europe's existing civic institutions are exclusionary and fail to harness the true potential of the communities in which they operate."

They define a civic entrepreneur as:

> ...someone who dares to be entrepreneurial in the part of society that most needs it: our communities. Where people see gridlock and problems, civic entrepreneurs see opportunity and mobilise their communities on a forward path. Their recipe is to forge powerfully productive linkages at the intersection of business, government, education, and community, thus helping to generate new innovative civic institutions, practices and social norms. By operating at the grassroots level, they create collaborative advantages that empower their communities to compete on the world stage.

Pulse of Europe is an example of civic entrepreneurialism, according to Alemanno and Cottakis. Founded in 2016, this citizen's initiative aims at counteracting Euroscepticism and "encouraging citizens of the European Union to speak out publicly in favour of a pan-European identity".

It is clear that social and civic entrepreneurship are interlinked. Both need to have at least an indirect impact on the political system, if they are to achieve their goals.

1.4   Political Entrepreneurship

The term "Political Entrepreneurship" isn't new, but there is, as yet, no generally accepted definition. It has various meanings in the political sciences, economics and sociology. Christian Hederer's useful overview ("Political entrepreneurship and institutional change: an evolutionary perspective", EAEPE Paper, November 2007), starts with Joseph Schumpeter.

In his 1942 book "Capitalism, Socialism and Democracy" (Harper Perennial Modern Classics, 2008), Schumpeter introduced the idea of entrepreneurship as innovation under conditions of fundamental uncertainty. The sources of economic progress, he claimed, are unexpected, rapid bursts of entrepreneur-driven growth. Entrepreneurs innovate by entering and disrupting markets. By creating something new, they destroy the value of incumbents with monopoly power ("creative destruction"). Because there are often significant barriers to market entry, new entrants have to be very different.

Schumpeter also saw democracy as a contest for market leadership. To him, a representative democracy was a constant leadership competition, not unlike the fight for market share. Whoever gets to lead, has the power to change political institutions and the public sector.

According to Hederer, most contemporary literature on Political Entrepreneurship "relates the concept to some notion of institutional innovation and/or innovation in the public sector, thereby following the Schumpeterian tradition".

Robert Dahl coined the term "political entrepreneur" in his seminal study of local politics in New Haven, in the US ("Who Governs? Democracy and Power in an American City", Yale University Press, 1961). He saw political entrepreneurs as "cunning, resourceful, masterful leaders" who brought about local change.

Adam Sheingate broadened Dahl's idea, by defining political entrepreneurs as "individuals whose creative acts have transformative effects on politics, policies, or institutions" ("Political Entrepreneurship, Institutional Change, and American Political Development", *Studies in American Political Development*, 2003). M. Schneider and P. Teske saw political entrepreneurs as "individuals who change the direction and flow of politics" ("Toward a Theory of the Political Entrepreneur: Evidence from Local Government", *American Political Science Review*, 1992). Others have defined political entrepreneurs as individuals running for office ("The Political Entrepreneur and the Coordination of the Political Process: A Market Process Perspective of the Political Market", François Abel, *Review of Austrian Economics*, 2003; "Political Entrepreneurship and Bidding for Political Monopoly." Michael Wohlgemuth, *Journal of Evolutionary Economics*, 2000).

Definitions of Political Entrepreneurship have not been confined to the political arena in the narrow sense. Randall Holcombe saw political entrepreneurs as individuals who act on political profit opportunities. "These profit opportunities can be divided into two categories: productive, and predatory. Productive opportunities enable entrepreneurs to profit from enhancing the efficiency of government, while predatory opportunities enable entrepreneurs to profit from forcibly transferring resources from some to others" ("Political Entrepreneurship and the Democratic Allocation of Economic Resources", *The Review of Austrian Economics*, 2002). As Baumol said of all entrepreneurs (op. cit.), Holcombe said political entrepreneurs can have positive or negative impacts on society.

The debate on Political Entrepreneurship is lively, but has yet to leave the academic realm: a Google search for the term "Political Entrepreneurship" in May 2018 returned 36,000 hits, compared to the 5.3 million for "Social Entrepreneurship".

The concept of Political Entrepreneurship developed in this book is novel, narrow, grounded and true to its Schumpeterian roots. It is most closely linked to the definitions of Sheingate, and Schneider and Teske (see above), but takes them a step further.

Where Sheingate sees "individuals whose creative acts have transformative effects on politics, policies, or institutions", I define political entrepreneurs as individuals whose main creative acts are *to found and develop political start-ups.*

Where Schneider and Teske see "individuals who change the direction and flow of politics", I define political entrepreneurs as those who do so *by founding and developing political start-ups, with the aim of entering parliament and transforming political systems from within.*

1.4.1   The Centrist Spring: Introducing the Political Start-Ups

One swallow doesn't make a Spring, as they say in England, but if you see seven swallows, you can be pretty sure that Winter is over.

My emphasis on start-ups in the debate about the meaning of the term "political entrepreneur" is based on my belief that the most important long-term political development in Europe is not the polarisation of democracies, but the emergence of new political parties of the centre. This book is based on more than 40 interviews with the leaders of six centrist political start-ups in Europe and one in Israel. They are:

Ciudadanos (https://www.ciudadanos-cs.org)
Founded in Catalonia in July 2006, the liberal political start-up entered the national stage of Spanish politics in 2015, winning 13.9% of the vote. They re-entered Parliament in the 2016 elections with 13.1% of the vote. In the Catalan regional elections of December 2017, they topped the polls with 25.4%. At the time of writing in August 2018, they are tied for second place in national opinion polls.

La République En Marche! (https://en-marche.fr)
Founded in April 2016 by Emmanuel Macron, who was elected President of France in May 2017. The centrist political start-up won 350 of the 577 seats in the French National Assembly election in June 2017. Together, these results transformed the political landscape of France.

Momentum Mozgalom (https://momentum.hu/)
Founded in March 2017, after they had defeated the bid for the Summer Olympics of Viktor Orban's Fidesz Government in January as a civil organisation. In April 2018, they failed to enter the Hungarian Parliament at their first attempt, winning 3.1% of the vote.

NEOS (https://www.neos.eu/)
Founded in October 2012, NEOS is a liberal political start-up that entered the Austrian Parliament in 2013 with 5.0% of the vote, and re-entered in 2017 with 5.3%. By 2018, NEOS was represented at all levels of government, including five of the nine state legislatures. In June 2018, it entered its first governing coalition in the state of Salzburg.

Nowoczesna (https://www.nowoczesna.org/)
Founded in May 2015, the liberal political start-up entered the Polish Parliament in October of that year with 7.6%, winning 28 of the 460 seats in the Sejm (the lower house of the Polish parliament). Following controversial reforms by the Law and Justice-Government, they polled as the strongest opposition party for all of 2016. In 2017, following some internal conflicts, there was a change of leadership.

Progresívne Slovensko (https://www.progresivne.sk/)
Founded in November 2017 in Slovakia, the progressive liberal political start-up officially launched in January 2018. At the time of writing, they were polling around 4.5% for general elections due in 2020.

Yesh Atid (https://www.yeshatid.org.il/)
Founded in April 2012 in Israel, the liberal political start-up entered the Knesset in January 2013 with 14.3%, becoming the second-largest party. They joined the governing coalition, and returned to Parliament at the 2015 election with 8.8% of the vote. At the time of writing, they were polling as the second largest party in most opinion polls.

Those involved in all seven of these start-ups exemplify my definition of political entrepreneurs:

> Political entrepreneurs are individuals who found and scale political start-ups, with the aim of entering parliament and transforming political systems from within.

1.5 Conceptual Distinctions

In contrast to Social and Civic Entrepreneurship, entering a political start-up in an election with the objective of entering government, is an attempt to have a *direct* impact on the political system.

Unlike the established term of 'policy entrepreneurship', it is not just about taking opportunities to influence policies, which is to say the *content* of politics. As shown in Table 1.1, it is about transforming the political system *as a whole*.

Two further conceptual distinctions are important.

First, political *activism* may also aim to transform the political system as a whole, and has certainly done so time and again in the course of history. Just think, for example, of the Velvet Revolution in what used to be Czechoslovakia. But political activism does so from *outside* parliament, and tends to evaporate, if it does not take control of concrete institutions with powers to match—think of the Arab Spring in Egypt, or the Occupy movement. Political Entrepreneurship, in contrast, aims to transform the political system and its institutions from *within*, by competing in the political markets.

Table 1.1 Concepts of entrepreneurship by objective and direction

	Indirect	Direct
Transformation of political system	Social entrepreneurship	Political entrepreneurship
Impact on aspects of political system	Civic entrepreneurship	Policy entrepreneurship

Table 1.2 The developmental stages of the seven political start-ups

Founded	Ran	Entered parliament	Re-entered parliament	In government
Progresívne	Momentum	Nowoczesna	Ciudadanos	En Marche Yesh Atid (until 2015) NEOS (at regional level)

Table 1.3 Entrepreneurship versus political entrepreneurship

Entrepreneurship	Political entrepreneurship
A new good (...) or of a new quality of a good	A new party/a new quality of party
A new method of production	New methods of decision-making and policy production
The opening of a new market	Opening up the political arena for citizens
The conquest of a new source of supply of raw materials or half-manufactured goods	Tapping into fresh, untapped talent, often with an entrepreneurial track record New ways of (crowd-)sourcing raw or half-baked ideas
The breaking up of a monopoly position	The breaking up of a monopoly or duopolies in the political market

Second, a crucial difference between business and social enterprises on the one hand, and political enterprises on the other, are elections. A start-up might go public in an initial public offering, but it does so only once. A social enterprise might have a decisive date where it pitches to its investors, but those investors are not all of the eligible voters in the country. Therefore, as Nicole Bolleyer argues in her seminal study on "New Parties in Old Systems" (Oxford University Press, 2013), political elections are an important marker to differentiate the stages of political start-ups, as is participation in government. The start-ups portrayed in this book can therefore be classified as shown in Table 1.2.

There is an important difference between improving existing parties, and founding new ones, in the same way as an incremental improvement of an existing technology or product differs from genuine, transformational novelty. Many of the founders of political start-ups tried and failed to transform existing parties before they took the risk of striking out on their own.

Returning to Schumpeter's five forms of innovation, the political entrepreneurs and their political start-ups portrayed in this book are innovative in some or all the Schumpeterian dimensions, as Table 1.3 shows.

1.5.1   Insiders Versus Outsiders

Another important distinction is between political start-ups founded by political insiders and political outsiders. As Nicole Bolleyer shows, in contrast to political start-ups on the left and right, most centrist political start-ups between 1968 and 2011 were founded by insiders, such as members of parliament of an existing party who defect and establish a spin-off. As I show in this book, however, a growing number of centrist political start-ups are being founded by political outsiders. This outsider quality lies at the heart of the phenomenon I am describing.

As Ivan Stefunko of Progressive Slovakia observed: "When Macron launched En Marche, he was in a different situation—he was quite visible, a Minister in the Hollande cabinet, who then created a kind of spin-off. For us, it is really a movement from the ground; 98% of our people have never been in politics. For 15 years I had no involvement in politics. So I can call myself a half-virgin in this sphere. We're more comparable to Momentum in Hungary, for example."

1.5.2   Rooted Versus Entrepreneurial

Bolleyer also differentiates political start-ups by their origins: if they receive significant support from organisations such as unions, employer organisations, environmental or religious groups, or other civil society organisations, Bolleyer calls them "rooted". If they're established from scratch, without this kind of support, she calls them "entrepreneurial".

". . . in the formative phase" Bolleyer explained, "we can specify whether or not a 'party in the making' can draw on linkages to societal groups which pre-date the party's formation. If a party can rely on such linkages, it will be referred to as a '*rooted new party*'. If it is created by individuals who are not affiliated to any already organised societal groups, it will be referred to as an '*entrepreneurial new party*'."

Traditionally, political start-ups on the left and right have tended to be "rooted" in this sense, whereas liberal and centrist political start-ups have tended to be founded from scratch. In the past these entrepreneurial new parties often relied on parliamentary insiders, as described above, instead of on civil society. While that also applies to the political start-ups in this book, I will argue later that tapping into and developing roots *after* starting-up is nonetheless important.

Bolleyer also differentiates political start-ups in terms of party formation: bottom up versus top-down. If local groups existed before the national organisation, the political start-up is classified as bottom-up. If the national organisation came first, then it is called top-down.

The political start-ups described in this book can be classified as shown in Table 1.4.

Table 1.4 Comparison of the political start-ups by founders and origins		Insider	Outsider
	Top-down	En Marche	Momentum NEOS Nowoczesna Progresívne Yesh Atid
	Bottom-up		Ciudadanos

Table 1.5 Comparison of the political start-ups based on media access

Access to mass media from outset	No access
Ciudadanos	Momentum
En Marche	NEOS
Nowoczesna	Progresívne
Yesh Atid	

1.5.3   Media Access

One final point to consider is whether or not a political start-up has access to mass media from the outset. As Bolleyer has shown, access to broadcasting is critical to the success of political start-ups. Having a public platform from the beginning is a real game-changer.

Ryszard Petru was a well-known academic who had been on TV many times before he launched Nowoczesna in Poland. Emmanuel Macron announced his plans while in office as Economics Minister. Yair Lapid had been one of Israel's best known TV anchor-men. That stage they were already standing on, and the access they already had, helped them to spread the word and catch the public's eye.

Having a celebrity as frontrunner helps, but it is not enough to build a sustainable political movement, as many failed political enterprises can attest to. In fact, too strong a focus on one person may ultimately lead to a less resilient organisation—in business, this is called the "Founder's Trap". And although a celebrity centre stage makes things easier, it is certainly possible to enter Parliament without one.

The political start-ups portrayed in this book can be classified as follows in Table 1.5.

1.6   Congratulations, It's a Start-Up!

What about the practical aspects of *entrepreneurship* in Political Entrepreneurship? Start-ups in the business and social spheres don't have the election cycles that put the quality of a political start-up to the test on one make-or-break day every 4 or 5 years, and they don't have to "sell" their products/policies to the mass market from the outset. But as an entrepreneur who has founded, led, and successfully sold a business start-up and has also worked in a social enterprise, I can attest to the wide array of attributes that political start-ups share with their cousins. Let's look at ten of them.

Believe in Yourself
"Advocating for new systems often required demolishing the old way of doing things, and we hold back for fear of rocking the boat", wrote Adam Grant in "Originals" (op. cit.). Do you want to rock the boat you're sailing on? People in your personal and professional circles might wonder why you would do that to yourself. They might be wondering why you are doing it to *them*. They might think your small act of resistance is futile. They might think you're a dreamer when you think big, and talk about transforming the system. Founding a political start-up is a

good way to lose clients and friends, and alienate lots of people. This is why political entrepreneurs, like all entrepreneurs, need to have a robust and stable sense of confidence and self-esteem that helps them to keep their feet on the ground, in times of failure as much as in times of success. Sometimes, however, overconfidence may turn into hubris, as I illustrate later in the book. Smart people do stupid things, and make unforced errors. At times, political entrepreneurs seem to be their own worst enemies in working towards their downfall. Their unwavering belief in themselves is as much a weakness as an essential strength.

Mentors and Sparring Partners

Even the very confident grapple at times with fear, doubt and ambivalence, and they too require a sanctuary. Even the most reflective intellect has its blind spots. This is why political entrepreneurs, like all entrepreneurs, need understanding mentors, who have relevant experience they can share, who can light the way, and who can provide solace or encouragement after a particularly taxing day. In addition, mentors and counsellors often provide access to crucial networks the political entrepreneur may lack.

Sparring partners are also critical to success. Early-stage ideas around the political start-up need vetting in a confidential environment, and trustworthy sparring partners can provide that. They may not necessarily be the best of friends, but they should be sympathetic to the cause, even though they might not join it. Most importantly, they are not afraid to state their views, and will not leak information to a third party.

Carving Out a Niche

Ignacio Lago and Ferran Martinez identified two key variables that explain the short term success of new political parties. First, the presence of electoral market failures, in the form of unsatisfied political demands shared by a significant number of voters in permissive electoral systems. Second, the number of elastic or "floating" voters willing to change their party allegiance if they receive a better offer—in other words, the degree of tribalism ("my party, right or wrong") in the party system affects the chances of new parties receiving sufficient votes to be viable ("Why new parties?" *Party Politics*, 2010).

As PayPal co-founder Peter Thiel wrote "you have to find a small market and monopolise it" ("Zero to One", *Currency*, 2014). In other words, you have to *avoid* competing with powerful incumbents. "Start small", however, is easier said than done. To become even a small player in the political market, you need to scout and sound out market opportunities constantly. You need to find your niche.

The key questions for political start-ups are: Who is currently not being represented? What political demands are unsatisfied? These are the questions Ciudadanos asked and answered in Catalonia in 2006: "There was a niche vote for a political party that was not nationalistic. There was a group of people who were not represented, and who didn't have a party representing that non-nationalistic interest or ideology."

Similarly, Ryszard Petru, founder of Nowoczesna in Poland, recalled what happened when Donald Tusk's Civic Platform government re-nationalised pension funds in 2013, when we talked at the ALDE congress in Amsterdam in December 2017: "people were suddenly queuing at the very last moment in front of the social security associations to choose between staying in the old system, leaving the public system, or keep paying part of their contribution to private pension funds.

I think there were half a million on one day, the last day of July—I think 2.5 million people chose the private pension funds. That showed the attitude of the people: 'We want to have a choice between private and public'. And I do remember I called a friend saying 'Listen, if 2.5 million want to have a choice...', this was the potential we had at first. It was a big number."

They made their bet, and won. Once you have made your bet, you need to focus your strategy, and polarise your messaging accordingly. After all, you have to polarise to mobilise.

Personal Life

Politics is intrusive and doubly so for a political start-up. After the daily grind and the evening talk-shows, you still have to fix the glitch in the database or amend the newsletter you want to send out the next morning. There is always *something*. Combine that with the addictive quality of politics, and you will find that partners and kids will at times find themselves fighting for attention, while you face cognitive overload.

Cross-Functional Work

Everyone does everything. In the beginning, there are no processes, or structures, but there's a huge opportunity and a major challenge. It is one of the reasons for that extra strain on your personal life. There is also no or little funding, and you have to work with the people you have. Chances are, those people do not possess all the requisite skills. There will be gaps and overlaps. The resulting constant collaborative improvisation, the "done is better than perfect" attitude, is what start-ups are about and what makes them nerve-racking for perfectionists.

Money

There is never enough money. And in markets flush with money, it is not enough to have the funding to operate—you need the funding to compete. Against the heavy hitters, respectively the large NGOs/companies/parties, the competition can sometimes seem unwinnable. Crowdfunding helps, but you may still need major donors to back you up. You might also need to put in some of your own money, or take out a loan. Putting your money where your mind is can be painful at times.

Partners

"If you want to go fast, go alone. If you want to go far, go together", says an African proverb. In business as in politics and the social sphere, entrepreneurs need alliances with key partners to realise their missions. Some of those partnerships might be of a strategic nature, like an electoral platform or a strategic consultancy relationship.

Other partnerships might be more operationally driven, like a buyer-supplier relationship to assure reliable supplies. In the end, both should serve to reduce risk and uncertainty, of which you have plenty anyway.

Magic Moments
And then, you win. The successful pitch to investors in your social enterprise, the IPO, the triumph on election day—it is hard to describe, and to overstate, the feeling of collective euphoria seeing something you helped to build with your own hands from scratch, succeed. It's a peak experience that comes with a high price. You may well have given it your all. Depression and burnout are the darker sides of the same coin.

Scale-Up or Consolidate
"Think big. Start small. *Scale fast.*" This is the start-up ethos. Scaling often needs a lot of resources that could also be used for some urgently needed investments. On the other hand, successful scaling-up can provide you with additional resources that are essential for achieving success in the medium and long terms. Scaling too fast can drain the start-up of the ability to maintain its core services. The organisation needs to be scaled in line with growth. That applies, first and foremost, to talent. There is also a need to keep reintegrating the organisation after each scaling, as it becomes increasingly complex. On the other hand, scaling too slowly can drain the start-up of the dynamic that keeps it alive.

Leadership
Leadership in start-ups is naturally more personality-focused than in established organisations. At the same time, if the entrepreneur wants to build a sustainable organisation, she or he has to help develop a culture and a structure that can survive a change at the top that will eventually occur, thus making such a change more likely. The entrepreneur has to make him- or herself genuinely replaceable. This is one of many dilemmas political entrepreneurs face, which are the subject of Chap. 3.

1.7   The Central Challenge

The seven political start-ups featured in this book are very different from each other in their origins, the manner of their birth, the environments in which they have entered or are entering their political arenas, their endowments in terms of their political experience and media access, their connections or lack of them with the institutions of civil society ("rootedness"), their strategies and objectives, their organisation, and their fund-raising abilities and achievements.

But these differences obscure a fundamental similarity. All these start-ups have been invoked by the vacuum at the centre of European politics. They speak with one voice to those who feel disenfranchised by the polarisation of their incumbent political parties. They, and similar centrist start-ups rumoured to be in the making in other countries, are putting a stake down in the centre ground and saying: "This is where we stand." They are showing that passionate political conviction is not confined to the ultra-left or ultra-right, that moderates can be militant too, and that the same energy, ingenuity, and optimism that is constantly refreshing the business world can give the silent, moderate majority new political choices.

How did it come to this? Why do we need these political start-ups? These are the questions to which I turn in the next chapter.

Liberal Democracies in Crisis

2

> *The democracy of our successors will not and cannot be the democracy of our predecessors. Nor should it be.*
> "Democracy and its Critics", Robert Dahl, Yale University Press (1991).

The modern era is an era of tectonic shifts that have put political systems under huge evolutionary pressure. The 2008 financial crisis and the migration crisis from 2015 are just the two most recent eruptions.

These crises have unfolded against the background of long-term trends that are also having an impact on our political systems, such as:

- climate change
- increasing speed of technological change
- global, but asymmetric population growth and concomitant migration
- asymmetric warfare
- the slow, but steady shift of economic power from west to east
- demographic change

Many of those challenges are continental and global in their impacts. Our current political architecture is not designed to deal with them effectively. The inherent inability of regional and national institutions to tackle those challenges leads to a blame game, where those accused of being responsible are either one level higher up (the capital/Brussels/the United Nations), or members of a clearly defined external group (the rich/migrants).

This is a game that populists, authoritarians, and extremists play very well. The closing decades of the twentieth century saw a global rise of democracies, but "progress has slowed over the past decade and, in some countries, it has halted

© Springer Nature Switzerland AG 2019
J. Lentsch, *Political Entrepreneurship*,
https://doi.org/10.1007/978-3-030-02861-9_2

completely" ("The Global State of Democracy: Exploring Democracy's Resilience", a report by the International Institute for Democracy and Electoral Assistance, 2017).

In the 2018 edition of its "Freedom in the World" ranking, Freedom House is even more pessimistic: the year "marked the 12th consecutive year of decline in global freedom." ("Freedom in the World", 2018). During that period, 112 countries saw a net decline in democracy, while only 62 experienced a net improvement. The edition is aptly called "Democracy in Crisis". Rights and freedoms we have learned to take for granted suddenly seem under threat, even inside the European Union.

Democracies are not only under threat, they are also under attack. Authoritarian regimes that want to weaken Western democracies deploy fake news to undermine their opinion-forming processes, and mount cyber attacks on their democratic systems and infrastructure.

Fittingly, the 2018 version of the Edelman Trust Barometer, a yearly online survey in 28 countries, is entitled "The Battle for Truth" ("2018 Edelman Trust Barometer"). Media are now the least trusted institutions, on a par with governments. A majority of citizens distrust both. It has become commonplace that "politician" is among the least trusted professions—in several countries, it is actually *the* least trusted. As an international survey of the French Fondation Pour l'Innovation Politique (FONDAPOL) from 2017 shows, in the European Union 87% agree with the statement "most politicians are mainly interested in protecting their own interests", and see politicians as corrupt. Political organisations fare no better. A disturbing third of the respondents do not see democracy as irreplaceable.

While liberal democracy has proved resilient since the end of World War II, given the pressures it has been subjected to, its survival in the twenty-first century seems far from guaranteed. In May 2018, Viktor Orban, starting his fourth term as Hungarian prime minister, declared "the era of liberal democracy" to be over.

In this battle for survival, proportional representation systems in continental Europe seem to be just as fragile and vulnerable as majority-rule systems in UK and the US. "Western Liberalism" as a whole seems to be in retreat. As Edward Luce wrote in his book "The Retreat of Western Liberalism" (Little, Brown, 2017):

> For centuries, Westerns have taken a linear view of history, in which time is always marching us towards a happier place. The Greeks called it teleology. For Christians, it was the Second Coming of Christ and the Day of Judgement. For Marxists, it was the dictatorship of the proletariat followed by the withering of the state. For European nationalists, it was seizing the control of their Volk destiny. For Georgian and Victorian liberals on both sides of the Atlantic, and their modern heirs across the Western world, it was the progress of human liberty and individual freedom. In 1989 most people believed the last version. The others were either dead or in retreat. Today, only Marxism remains dormant. Belief in an authoritarian version of national destiny is staging a powerful comeback. Western liberalism is under siege.

Authoritarian versions of national destiny come in different shapes and sizes, such as Hungary's "illiberal democracy" or Russia's "hybrid democracy", but all share a desire to roll-back two of liberal democracy's greatest achievements: individual rights and the rule of law.

The most venerable democracies are not immune to the rise of populism; witness the success of the Brexit campaign in the UK and Donald Trump's victory in the 2016 US Presidential election. Shocked observers may have looked in the wrong places. As Pankaj Mishra has pointed out, "GDP numbers insist we are doing well, at a time when half the country is suffering from personal recessions." The malaise goes even deeper: "People have lost faith that their systems can deliver. ... When a culture stops looking for the future, it loses a vital force" ("The Age of Anger", Allen Lane, 2017).

The result said Mishra, quoting Hannah Arendt, is a "'tremendous increase in mutual hatred and a somewhat universal irritability of everybody against everybody', or 'ressentiment.' An existential resentment of other people's being, caused by an intense mix of envy and a sense of humiliation and powerlessness."

If anything, proportional representation systems seem more vulnerable to the rise of populist or extremist parties, many of them founded recently, like the Alternative für Deutschland in Germany, the Movimento 5 Stelle in Italy, the People's Party in Slovakia or the PVV in the Netherlands. The observed fragmentation of political systems further weakens the capacity of the parties within them to act.

The disintegration of traditional political parties may be as much a driver, as a consequence of the democratic downward spiral, according to Uri Friedman ("What if the 'Populist Wave' is just political fragmentation?", *The Atlantic*, March 17, 2017). Traditional parties on the centre right and centre left are either "at war with themselves", due to ideological infighting, as in the UK and the US, as Dean Burnett argues ("Why political parties fall apart: the psychology of infighting", *The Guardian*, 21 Mar 21, 2016), or they keep losing members, and continue to cede vote share to the populists and extremists at the fringes of the political spectrum, as in several European countries, most recently in Italy.

A big part of this problem are traditional centrist parties themselves. As Mishra put it: "When elites appear ineffective, voters give radicals a chance." In other words, if centrists are unable or unwilling to deliver much-needed reforms, voters give institution-smashers a go, with potentially disastrous consequences.

Traditionally, centre right parties in particular have acted as gatekeepers, and have kept authoritarians and populists at bay, as Steven Levitsky and Daniel Ziblatt argue in their book "How Democracies Die" (*Crown*, 2018). Today, however, it is often the centre right itself that becomes increasingly authoritarian, as in Poland, or switches from gatekeeper to door opener to the far right, as in Austria. "Democratic backsliding begins at the ballot box" as Levitsky and Ziblatt put it.

Even where the centre right still draws a line between itself and the far right, the line is getting progressively thinner. "It is not what extremists say that threatens Europe", writes the political scientist Ivan Krastev in his essay "After Europe", "the real threat is what the mainstream leaders no longer say" (*Combined Academic Publishing*, 2017). Or, as the Anglo-Irish statesman Edmund Burke is supposed to have said: "The only thing necessary for the triumph of evil is for good men to do nothing."

Some say that, as a consequence of all this, liberalism and democracy, which have complemented each other since World War II, are becoming detached. Yascha Mounk argues in "The People vs. Democracy" (*Harvard University Press*, 2018) that when populists take the reins, or when the centre right adopts parts of populist platforms, liberal institutions such as civil rights, the rule of law and the separation of powers are weakened to an alarming degree. This gives rise to "democracies without rights"—illiberal democracies as in Hungary. On the other hand, there is a growing sense at both ends of the spectrum that "political elites have insulated themselves from popular views", giving rise to "rights without democracy" where technocrats and bureaucrats rule instead of elected parliamentarians. According to Mounk: "Liberal democracy is now decomposing into its component parts—giving rise to illiberal democracy on the one side and undemocratic liberalism on the other".

The weakening of institutions further fans popular anger.

Are we on the road to Hobbes' State of Nature, to a *bellum omnium contra omnes*? Are our democracies in inexorable dystopian decline?

Political science is good at explaining the crisis and its manifold origins, but not so good at proposing remedies. More specifically, political scientists have been so preoccupied with populists and extremists that they have neglected the political centre. But the protagonists in this book prove that we in the political centre can do something to save liberal democracy, and re-invent politics for the twenty-first century.

The future is not set—for worse, or better. Regress is certainly possible, but so is progress.

2.1   Realignment Instead of Disintegration

The alternative narrative to the dystopian visions above goes like this: our liberal democracies are in transition. Systems destabilise before they evolve. That can be disturbing, sometimes deeply, but it is normal. Transitions to new equilibria are messy. They take time. And the new equilibrium may not even look like an equilibrium. We should not be scared of that.

As the MIT-based action researcher Otto Scharmer writes in "Theory U: Learning from the Future as it emerges" (Berrett-Koehler, 2009).

"The social structures that we see decaying and crumbling—locally, regionally and globally—are built on two different sources: pre-modern *traditional* and *modern* industrial structures or forms of thinking and operating. Both of them have been successful in the past. But in our current age, each disintegrates and crumbles."

The same applies to political structures and political forms of thinking and operating. Most of our Western democracies were designed in the early twentieth century, some even in the late eighteenth century. Democracies in post-Communist countries are of a significantly more recent origin, but are still based on a design that is 100 or more years old. True, that design has been wildly successful for quite some time now. But it has not yet been significantly updated to meet the twenty-first century challenges and needs. Consequently, liberal democracies are overstretched, and underperforming. That creates opportunities for political start-ups.

Take Spain. As Jorge Lobeto, one of the parliamentary advisers of Ciudadanos, told me, "it's 40 years since the first democratic election in Spain after the Franco dictatorship. And in those 40 years most of the time there were two main parties in power: the Socialist and the Popular Party (the conservatives), alternating between one and the other.

There was a kind of dissatisfaction in the people, especially with the territorial dispute [Catalonia and the Basque country]. And then some social issues. Because the socialist party was trying to move to the political centre to occupy all the space, that left people dissatisfied on the left wing. And both big parties left people dissatisfied with how they were managing the territorial issue. So these two axes created a space for a party in the centre."

In the quote at the beginning of this chapter, Robert Dahl, one of liberal democracy's wisest friends in the twentieth century, noted that our democracy will not and cannot be the democracy of our predecessors. So why should our political parties be the parties of our predecessors?

Perhaps the current political crisis is actually a turning point. The post-war Western order was dominated by what Maurice Duverger in 1951 called "Mass-based parties" (quoted in "Les partis politiques", Seuil, 1992)—with a large memberships, stable structures and strong hierarchies. They provided stability after chaos, and gave opposing factions within society the platforms on which to reconcile peacefully. Even in proportional representation systems, two mass-based parties often accounted for between 70 and 80% of the vote, above the two-thirds threshold required in many countries to change the constitution.

These mass-based parties were complemented by "Elite-based parties", which were more flexible, but typically relied more on charismatic leaders, and were, for that reason, less stable.

In many cases, post-war stability has turned into ossification, caution has turned to inaction, strong hierarchies have turned into authoritarian tendencies, elites have turned into self-serving establishments, and trust-based politics has turned into systemic corruption.

In various long-standing democracies, political markets have become duopolies of two major parties, or oligopolies of a few that haven't changed much since World War II. The fragile post-communist political markets, on the other hand, seem to have attracted ghosts from their pasts.

The populists of the right and left sense their opportunity. They channel the rage against the political establishment, or alternatively against "the other". And they do it quite well: "For the first time since the Second World War, liberal democracy no longer seems to be the only option for Western societies" said historian Philipp Blom in his keynote address to the first European Innovation in Politics Awards in December, 2017. "It is true that the dismay of some... reveals a degree of egotism: the current order is serving them rather well; they feel entitled to maintain it, and they are prepared to close ranks to protect the interests of their own perceived 'tribe'." But there are also many others, equally dismayed, whose concerns are broader. These people care about reforming the system, while preserving the good enshrined in it.

When democracy can no longer guarantee the fundamental values on which it is built, incremental change will not do. Liberal democracy is in need of disruption. The thrust for this disruption cannot come from the traditional political parties when they themselves are part of the system. As Albert Einstein said: "we cannot solve our problems with the same level of thinking that created them." But it is far from inevitable that the consequences of such disruption will be to the liking of centrists. The populist challenge may have been fended off for now, but it is certainly far from over.

We therefore need new actors to help bring about real, positive transformation. This requires constructive alternatives to the populists and extremists. New parties in the political centre are needed. Some of them are the stars of this book.

Whether the upcoming democratic disruption will lead to decline or innovative transformation will be decided in a race—the race between political entrepreneurs at the political extremes, and those in the political centre. To win this race, the latter will need to reinvent the political centre.

For that, Edward Luce writes, "liberal elites, in particular, will have to resist the temptation to carry on with their comfortable lives and imagine doing their part by signing up to the occasional Facebook protest" (op. cit.).

They need to leave the stands, and enter the arena as the courageous protagonists in this book have already done.

We are entering an era of political experimentation. It's a frightening thought in an environment that is highly volatile, uncertain, complex and ambiguous. Failure is a possibility. At the same time, learning from failure is the only way forward. To paraphrase the Austrian-born American educator and author Peter Drucker, political entrepreneurs eat failure for breakfast.

2.2 Reclaiming Democracy

"Politics seems to be the thing to care for", Daniel Kruse, one of the initiators of the Open State of Politics, a German conference for envisioning a new politics, told me in Berlin in the Summer of 2017. The sentence stuck with me. "The thing to care for" made politics sound precious, vulnerable, even endangered. In the past couple of decades, the thing to care for might have been the social sphere. Now it is politics.

In "Reclaiming Democracy: A Plea for Political Entrepreneurship" (Stanford Social Innovation Research, October, 2013) Lisa Witter and Catherine de Vries identify five interrelated phenomena that comprise the challenge facing democracies:

- complexity
- political short-sightedness
- unaccountability
- the decline of political parties
- a talent deficit in politics

They saw "a crisis of political representation and accountability throughout the advanced industrial world and emerging markets". If anything, this crisis has deepened since 2013.

Their analysis led Witter and de Vries to call for a "Political Entrepreneurship Movement" (Witter has since then become an Entrepreneur herself, and founded the Apolitical, a global network for government innovation):

> Can a group of political entrepreneurs fighting for sustainability in nature, schools, streets, workplaces, or the marketplace reclaim the political arena and ignite enthusiasm for politics? If we truly care about the state of our world, democracy, and economy, the answer must be yes. If so, the question becomes how? How can political entrepreneurs develop new modes of citizen-politics linkage, and develop policies that work and solve the problems we face? Who are these entrepreneurs? Where are they, and what can we do to excite, support, and engage them in change?

They see the need for a transformation of the political system, and suggest what such a change should look like:

- Politics through people: more talent, fewer tribes
- Evidence-based public policy: more evidence, less ideology
- Open and accountable politics: more transparency, less strategy
- Popping the cynicism bubble and crowdsourcing solutions

They conclude their academic *cri de coeur* with a call for the formation of an international collaborative community of political entrepreneurs, building on the experience of the Social Entrepreneurship movement.

Witter and de Vries were ahead of their time. As Nicole Bolleyer had shown, there weren't many centrist political start-ups of the kind they yearned for at the time. There are now. The ideas of Witter and de Vries are as relevant as ever and lie at the heart of centrist Political Entrepreneurship.

Political Entrepreneurship is new people, founding new parties in new ways. But even more importantly, it is about transforming political systems through those new people, new parties and new methods. This transformation can be understood as *re-purposing* political systems. This goes far beyond simply fighting and winning in the political arena, although that is an integral part of it. It aims to reinvent and reconstruct the political arena as a whole. This requires "Leading from the emerging future", as Otto Scharmer called it in "Theory U" (op. cit.).

But not all political entrepreneurs are on what centrists would regard as the side of the angels. Howard Stevenson's definition of entrepreneurs cited at the beginning of this chapter is morally neutral. So is the definition of political entrepreneurs. They include anyone, including populists and extremists, who sees a political opportunity.

Some of the most successful recent examples of political entrepreneurs are populists and extremists in Europe. With their new parties on the right (e.g. PVV, UKIP and AfD) and left (e.g. Podemos and, to some extent, Movimento 5 Stelle), they have managed to capture large political market shares.

The political entrepreneurs I am focusing on in this book are the founders of new centrist parties that try to enter parliaments, positively disrupt our democracies, and reinvent the political centre. They try to beat the new populists and extremists by being "better" political entrepreneurs, by which I mean being better at the politics and better at the entrepreneuring.

Political entrepreneurs are citizens who aim to transform political systems, by creating new, innovative parties, to address society's most pressing problems. At best, they are productive (or creatively destructive). At worst, they're simply destructive. Either way, they hold the key to the future of our democracies.

2.3   Resourceful Revolutionaries

Centrist political entrepreneurs may not be revolutionaries from the outset. Often, they first try to get traditional parties to reform. Ryszard Petru advised the Civic Platform, Matthias Strolz advised the ÖVP, Emmanuel Macron was a minister in the cabinet of a socialist president.

It is a common misconception that entrepreneurs are reckless risk takers. On the contrary: entrepreneurs usually strive to minimise risk, because they know the risks of failure. "The best entrepreneurs are not risk maximisers. They take the risk out of risk-taking", said Endeavour CEO, Linda Rottenberg (quoted in "Originals: How Non-Conformists Move the World", Adam Grant, Viking, 2016). Learning from failure is central to any entrepreneurial undertaking. As Samuel Beckett put it: "Ever tried. Ever failed. No matter. Try Again. Fail again. Fail better." This is how political entrepreneurs succeed.

All political entrepreneurs are political animals in one way or another, but being a political animal is a long way from being a political entrepreneur. There may be no unique point of transition from the former to the latter, but there are often episodes, incidents and encounters that, in hindsight, are seen as emotional or intellectual epiphanies.

"I was invited to the education group of the ÖVP [the conservative Austrian People's Party] a couple of times." Matthias Strolz, one of the co-founders of NEOS, told me. "I liked that; not being there as consultant, but as an expert. University presidents were there and others who I had not known were affiliated. The Minister for Higher Education said he had to know whether teachers in the Gymnasiums and the Hauptschule (as the lower secondary from year 5 to 8 is called in Austria) should be trained jointly or separately in the future [they were separate at the time]. I had a hard time watching the debate; 60 smart people, and not one opened his or her mouth."

"At one point, I got up and said: 'Sorry, I am only an advisor, but I cannot keep quiet any longer, because the thing is crystal clear. It is the same curriculum, and the same age group—if the ÖVP takes the stand that training and remuneration need to be kept separate, to keep up the stigmatisation particularly of those young people in the Hauptschule, then you deserve to be called *Bildungsbetonierer* [education reform blockers]. There is no intellectual reason to keep it like that!' And then someone next to me whispered in my ear: 'Our thoughts exactly.' And I asked: 'So why don't you voice them?' I got no reply. Then, right after me, two teacher union representatives made the case for keeping the two streams separate. And I knew, I am out of here. I do not belong here."

The episode illustrates a certain Lutheran quality of political entrepreneurs: "Here I stand; I can do no other."

2.4   The Importance of Roots

As noted in Chap. 1, Nicole Bolleyer distinguishes in "New Parties in Old Systems" (op. cit.) between "rooted" and "entrepreneurial" political start-ups. "Rooted" start-ups can rely on significant support from civil society or business associations, while "entrepreneurial" start-ups are built independently from scratch. Most political start-ups on the Left, are "rooted", whereas liberal and centrist political start-ups tend to be entrepreneurial. Historically, that has affected their long-term survival rate, as Bolleyer has shown for parties founded between 1968 and 2011. Roots help.

Roots become particularly important after the political start-up enters parliament. As Bolleyer showed, "coping with the challenges of institutionalisation and the pressures of public office after breakthrough, is easier for rooted newcomers."

Roots are, in that sense, a competitive advantage for a political start-up. Roots can give a start-up resilience. Political entrepreneurs can compensate for a lack of roots, however, by making smart choices, such as building strategic alliances or tapping into networks in civil society.

For NEOS, one such reservoir was the Platform for Open Politics (POP), a civic association founded in 1995. The Platform had two main visions: a more liberal, modern and cosmopolitan politics, and a more participative politics. In short: liberalism and participation. At the time NEOS was founded in 2012, the platform was inactive. But POP's agenda lived on, not only on its website, which remains active to this day, but much more importantly, in its inner circle of promoters, some of whom later joined the founding group of NEOS.

Another reservoir was youth organisations. While they did not evolve out of them, En Marche, NEOS and Nowoczesna all have youth organisations, or youth organisations aligned with them, that predate them.

Young people are at the centre of today's democratic crises. In many societies, the young are hit hardest by unemployment, face a less secure future, and will have to shoulder the public debts being incurred today. Youth organisations are, therefore, the roots of political transformation.

"They fulfil an important function as contact points for politically interested youth", Niki Scherak, former Chairman of the Austrian JuLis ("Young Liberals"), told me when I spoke with him in Vienna in December, 2017. In 2014, after they successfully entered Parliament on an electoral platform with NEOS and the Liberal Forum, they changed their name to JUNOS ("Young Liberal NEOS"), and became the youth organisation of NEOS. "Also, you learn about the architecture of political processes, and get used to a certain sequencing of collective decision-making." This helps particularly in the early days of a political enterprise, when everything is new to almost everyone.

They may also learn how to speak publicly and campaign effectively: for example, in Austria, every 2 years students vote in student councils, ranging from individual university departments, to a national council. In these elections, JUNOS run their own campaign, under their own banner—a perfect training and recruiting ground for future parliamentarians and senior political staff. Several of NEOS's founding board members were involved in student politics while at university.

The young are fresh talent as well as future leaders. They are the new heads required to envision a new politics, and bring it to life. They are often more idealistic, and also more ideological than their more experienced colleagues, and will come up with fresher, and more radical ideas than those emanating from the "mothership". That is a good thing, because those who have been socialised in a political system for decades might find it harder to disengage themselves from it intellectually, and be positive about a vision of politics that looks very different. Young people are also generally well-educated and internationally minded, which helps them to think outside the national box.

Take Miłosz Hodun, now working as an expert at the Nowoczesna headquarters in Warsaw. He holds a PhD and is a former part-time lecturer at Reykjavik University School of Law. His main areas of interest are comparative constitutional law and federalism. He is a board member of "Projekt: Polska", an association he co-founded in 2005 as a youth project. The first "liberal, interdisciplinary think tank" in Poland, Projekt: Polska branched out all over Poland. It gathered together many young intellectuals and political animals and became an invaluable source of talent and know-how for Nowoczesna.

Projekt: Polska emerged from the ashes of the former Polish liberal party "Unia Wolności" (The Freedom Union), founded in 1994 by distinguished politicians such as Tadeusz Mazowiecki, Leszek Balcerowicz and Bronisław Geremek. Unia Wolności became a large opposition party in 1997, lost out in 2001, and was dissolved in 2005. Hodun was in his early twenties when the party died. Together with other former members of the Unia Wolności youth wing, he decided to create Projekt: Polska. "We changed the name, because we didn't want it to be party-affiliated", Hodun told me during our interview in Warsaw in February, 2017. "After all, there was no party."

Project: Polska grew to 300–400 members in 20 branches all over Poland. It became a highly recognised NGO, one of the largest after the Church and the Scouts. During all this time, they were supported by the German liberal Friedrich Naumann Foundation for Freedom. "For us, Projekt: Polska was this, I don't know, little hive that keeps people together, to learn from each other", said Hodun. "We were also stating in our manifesto that we wanted to train good staff for future political administrations, in all aspects of it. We wanted to train public servants, but also politicians and teachers, give them liberal values, and have them stick together."

Their success emboldened them to open their doors to more experienced people—liberal 40-year-olds who had been in their twenties in the early 1990s, when many of them had worked in the first government of Tadeusz Mazowiecki. They had been the young assistants of ministers at the very beginning of the Polish post-communist transformation.

Some of these 40-year-olds had well-established companies and good incomes, and wanted to do something for society. They joined forces with the young, put in some money and helped create the "Projekt: Polska Foundation" in addition to the existing association. The foundation raised funds and acted as a think-tank that designed civil society campaigns. The association used its network to conduct these campaigns all over the country, particularly targeting younger people. A new nation-wide supply chain for developing and implementing political ideas emerged.

A major Projekt: Polska project was a series of civil society events in 2004 to commemorate the 15th anniversary of the fall of Communism. They managed to gather some 300 organisations and jointly staged thousands of events all over the country. Adam Szłapka ran the whole process. Ten years later, he become the General Secretary of the liberal political start-up, Nowoczesna.

Young people help political start-ups develop new ideas. Students are also crucial for mobilisation, because they can more easily make time to campaign. Ludovic Bain, a student at the Sorbonne who leads field actions for Les Jeunes avec Macron, told me the youth organisation was "the 'armed forces' of En Marche."

Youth organisations not only help political enterprises enter parliament. They're just as valuable after the new party has entered parliament, or in the case of En Marche, government, as "thorns in the side" of the mother party's members that keep them honest and hold them to account for their pre-election promises.

It is important to have a clear and stable relationship between the youth organisation and the mother party, whether it's relatively distant, as in the case of Projekt: Polska and Nowoczesna, or close as in the cases of Jeunes avec Macron and En Marche, and JUNOS and NEOS. It is also important to review the relationship regularly and allow it to evolve as changing circumstances require.

Youth organisations have a special position that must be defended against members who doubt the value their internal influence and importance. At the same time, their positions need to be open to challenge and scrutiny, just as everything else in a political enterprise.

The youth organisation must on no account become a reactionary force. It can happen. Hungary's populist party, Fidesz, started out as a hopeful liberal youth party with an upper age limit of 35. What this means in practice is that care should be taken to ensure the ability of the youth organisation to mobilise doesn't create a kind of "party within the party", with its own policies or legislative programme. But care must be taken to ensure that reining in at times ideologically over-zealous young people doesn't alienate them.

The youth organisation must not become a group with a vested interest by, for example, giving them quotas on the lists, but by the same token, the main party must not exploit the youth organisation's mobilisation ability. It should be respected as a relevant voice. It is in the interests of the party to recognise, empower and develop young talent, and to include youth representatives on its strategic boards.

Friction between the youth organisation and the mother party, while they remain strategically aligned, is essential. A political party that doesn't debate and argue internally is a dead party. A balance must be struck. At best, the relationship is mutually challenging and invigorating at the same time. The successful management of such a delicate relationship is one of many leadership challenges political entrepreneurs face. I will delve into them in the next chapter.

Leadership

3

> *The most authentic political leadership is to be seen when large numbers of people are inspired by someone who has neither power nor patronage to dispose of, but whose message strikes a chord with them. Such leadership can be provided by an emergent or rising political party, by a group, or by an individual. It is the readiness of others that defines the effectiveness of such political leadership.*
> Archie Brown, "The Myth Of The Strong Leader: Political Leadership in the Modern Age" (Basic Books, 2014).

As Michael Foley has pointed out: "Political leadership is a notoriously elusive and variable construct", which is consequently "susceptible to an intricate diversity of different interpretations and categories of associational life" ("Political Leadership: Themes, Contexts and Critiques", Oxford University Press, 2013). This chapter is not an attempt to bring order to Foley's diversity, but there are some constraints and conditions all political entrepreneurs face when aspiring to become political leaders or having leadership thrust upon them.

3.1 Without Power

As a political entrepreneur, you start with a blank slate. There is, as the Archie Brown-quote above dryly states, "neither power nor patronage to dispose of". To tap into "the readiness of others" with "a message that strikes a chord" is a great opportunity, and a great challenge. It also puts you in a precarious position. Once you strike a chord effectively, and rise above the threshold of public awareness, the system immediately deploys counter-measures that may hit you where it hurts professionally, or even privately.

© Springer Nature Switzerland AG 2019
J. Lentsch, *Political Entrepreneurship*,
https://doi.org/10.1007/978-3-030-02861-9_3

Once the Austrian Conservatives got word that NEOS was in the making, their then General Secretary told NEOS co-founder Matthias Strolz: "If you do that, you will be professionally and politically dead in 2 days". Even in stable democracies, traditional parties can act like the Mafia when they feel threatened. Strolz' company, which advised businesses and organisations in the private, public and the third sector, lost clients and projects. Others known to be involved with the founding were also sanctioned—the professional *famiglia* had struck. Ultimately, everyone is susceptible to blackmail. But of course, the less the political entrepreneur is beholden to the current political system in the first place, the better.

A lack of power doesn't mean a lack of leverage. Entrepreneurship is, as Howard Stevenson said, "the pursuit of opportunity beyond resources currently controlled" (see Sect. 1.1). Although political power may not be among them at the beginning of the journey, the political entrepreneur will take stock of the *resources currently controlled*.

Key resources controlled will include:

- **Social capital**—private and professional networks, good name and reputation.
- **Intellectual and practical capital**—knowledge and skills.
- **Financial capital**—yes, it helps.

The political entrepreneur has access not to power, but to sources of influence. In addition to the three "capitals" listed above, there are personal sources of influence, such as charisma, storytelling skill and being a role model. The latter may sometimes be a slow burner, but it is all the more influential in the long term: walking the talk, demonstrating again and again how a prototype of new politics can work in practice. That is authority through authenticity—real people, taking real risks, to bring about real change.

And in the midst of the "post-heroic politics" in the post-modern twenty-first century, there is clearly a heroic aspect to this. On a very personal level, authenticity provides credibility, but also means vulnerability.

Authenticity is one of the core values of NEOS. Together with appreciation, it builds the backbone of the espoused NEOS attitude. Right from the beginning, NEOS said part of its mission was to "bring a new style to Austrian politics". Authenticity was something that citizens missed in the political arena. But not only in politics: people have a basic need to connect with public personae—not just as voters, but also as human beings.

Authenticity, therefore, is a very practical dimension of the political entrepreneur who aspires to become a political leader. It is certainly not the only one. At a workshop of liberal parties in Madrid in November 2017, where Ciudadanos and NEOS participated, the following dimensions were deemed critical when looking for leadership talent:

- Political sensitivity
- Communication and networking skills
- Representative of the wider public

- Entrepreneurial approach
- Responsibility
- Strategic thinking and judgement
- Resilience

In his book "The Myth of the Strong Leader" (op. cit.), Archie Brown, lists some other leadership qualities:

> These include integrity, intelligence, articulateness, collegiality, shrewd judgment, a questioning mind, willingness to seek disparate views, ability to absorb information, flexibility, good memory, courage, vision, empathy and boundless energy. Although incomplete, this is already a formidable list. We should hardly expect most leaders to embody *all* of those qualities. They are not superwomen or supermen, and they should not forget it. . .

All of these qualities come without price tags attached to them, and can be exercised without pre-existing power.

Brown writes, correctly in my view, that "we should not expect [individual] leaders to embody *all* of those qualities". We should, however, expect leadership teams to embody most or all of them. Politics is a team sport. "You can't go anywhere in politics without a team who give their all", said Michael Ignatieff in "Fire and Ashes" (Harvard University Press, 2013), his highly readable account of his failed bid to become Prime Minister of Canada. Teams consist not only of players. They also have a particular strategy, structure and culture. Leadership, therefore, is not just about the quality of individual leaders. It's also about the quality of the people around them, and the organisation—its strategy, culture and structure—as a whole. Building a team, and developing an effective and viable organisation around it, and all of that from scratch, is one of the core challenges for political entrepreneurs.

3.2 In Uncertainty

"Leaders in politics need to have a strong inner compass", said Angelika Mlinar, at the time Deputy Chairwoman of NEOS, when I talked to her in Vienna in October 2017. "Unfortunately, too often they don't."

Toni Roldán Monés, the Director of Programme of Ciudadanos, takes a similar view: "I think you need to know very clearly what you want to do in politics. You cannot try to aim at 300 targets, because then you lose the true north."

It is an existential condition of any start-up, political or otherwise, that it operates in an extremely uncertain environment. But it's worse than that. The U.S. Army teaches its generals-in-waiting that modern battlefields and theatres of conflict are volatile, uncertain, complex and ambiguous (VUCA). It's the same with modern theatres of politics.

A firm sense of political mission, and sorted-out personal values—the "strong inner compass"—are also essential qualities for successful political entrepreneurs. After all, "the first thing you need to know when you enter politics is why you're doing it", said Michael Ignatieff (op. cit.). If you cannot answer the question in one simple sentence, with a sense of rage in your guts, don't do it.

Even if you can spell it out, the extreme uncertainty coupled with the competitiveness within the political arena make for a hostile environment. Most political start-ups never make it into parliament (in Austria, there are 1000 registered parties, only five of which are currently represented in the national Parliament).

Before you even get a chance to run, though, there are months or even years of time, energy and resources to invest. To date, there is no advance seed funding for political start-ups. You are either in parliament, or out of money (once you are in, however, depending on the political system you arguably have more financial security than private or third sector start-ups, which can seldom plan ahead for the next 4 or 5 years.)

The critical quality here is resilience; the ability to recover from or adjust easily to misfortune or change. One key pillar of resilience is maintaining communication and sharing information at all times, even if that means sharing the awareness of ignorance. As Stefan Egger, Managing Director of NEOS, put it: "In politics, leadership means conveying clarity. No matter in which role. Politics is about clarity internally as much as externally. The context is volatile—in 2013, every day was different. It is like on the high seas. You are sailing a relatively small boat on a large ocean, and you don't know whether tomorrow there will be a storm, an island, a pirate ship, or something else. You simply don't know, so you are better prepared. And that is what people feel. Whoever comes on board our ship feels he or she has lots of freedom, but also that there is little prospect of success. So we need to share the views we have with our people, and I think that's what we are good at. Sometimes that view does not carry far, a week or two, sometimes half a year, but sharing it helps people to process.

And you should not let a changing context lead you astray from your course. You will never know what the right call would have been. Were you too participative? Did you give too few parameters? Were you too authoritarian? Were you fair? If you have clarity for yourself, you can cope. If you don't, it gets difficult for everyone involved."

The key to resilience and clarity, on a personal level, is a mature, strong and stable ego. Contemporary politics with its public cock-fighting rituals, and media that encourage such behaviour, has a tendency to attract immature, weak and unstable egos who crave external validation. For them, politics is a drug. If they want to transform the system, political entrepreneurs must not get high on politics.

3.3   For the Greater Good

NEOS had just made Austrian history by entering Parliament on the first attempt in September 2013. It had run on an electoral platform with the Liberal Forum, a liberal party that had been created in a split-off from the then national-liberal Freedom Party in 1993. The electoral platform also included the JuLis (the Young Liberals, later to be renamed JUNOS—young liberal NEOS), who had split off from the Liberal Forum a couple of years earlier.

There are examples of such electoral platforms being successful at the voting booth around the world; there are fewer examples of platforms that remain successful *after* having been elected (the most notable exceptions being the Liberal-National Coalition in Australia, and, to a lesser extent, the CDU/CSU in Germany). The centrifugal forces take over, and differing interests lead to a crumbling of the electoral platform. So, after negotiating an agreement, NEOS and the Liberal Forum decided to merge. As this is not possible under Austrian Law, Angelika Mlinar, then Chairwoman of the Liberal Forum, agreed to what Nicole Bolleyer called "Death by strategic merger" (op. cit.): the Liberal Forum would merge *into* NEOS.

"It was a very emotional moment", Mlinar told me, when recalling the Merger Assembly in January, 2014, which saw the end of the Liberal Forum as a standalone party. "Also, in terms of power politics, I gave up a lot of power that day. But it was the right thing to do." She subsequently became President of NEOS Lab, Deputy Chairwoman of NEOS, Member of the European Parliament, and Vice-President of the Alliance of Liberals and Democrats for Europe.

In his book "Great by Choice", Jim Collins develops the concept of "Level 5 Ambition" (HarperBusiness, 2011). Those leaders, he writes, are "incredibly ambitious, but their ambition is first and foremost for the cause, for the company, for the work, not themselves."

They need to achieve results for a greater good rather than for themselves. They have the drive and passion to do whatever it takes to achieve those results, and continuously push to motivate and engage others in their quest. This is what leading for the greater good means: making tough choices in the common interest. That is what Mlinar and the members of the Liberal Forum did that day.

3.4 Without Clients

Stefan Egger, NEOS Executive Director, worked in the private sector with media and technology start-ups before entering politics. "The easy thing about management in politics is that you don't have clients" he told me. "Coming from the private sector, that is the main difference: clients don't trouble you any more. They're great, but they can also be pests.

On the other hand, you suddenly have thousands, tens of thousands or hopefully more 'stakeholders'. Voters, [party] members who are much more powerful, functionaries and representatives on all levels—they are all stakeholders. They all want something. They all have expectations. To keep a clear view of this game, and not take it personally, and to keep all the balls in the air, and to keep people motivated and to give them the freedom to act—that is, I think, the secret. But also to say 'here are the limits to this freedom'. Some can give freedom well, others can set limits well—the challenge is to combine both in yourself, leadership and stakeholder participation. That is the greatest challenge in political management."

Egger speaks here for all of us former business entrepreneurs. Political start-ups face environments that are just as complex as the business environment, but it is a different kind of complexity.

3.5   From the Future

"The crisis", wrote Antonio Gramsci in his Prison Notebooks, "consists precisely in the fact that the old is dying and the new cannot be born; in this interregnum a great variety of morbid symptoms appear." ("Selections from the Prison Notebooks", Lawrence and Wishart, 1971). We are living in such an interregnum. The present political system does not work any longer. How can we help the new to be born? How can we as political entrepreneurs cope with these shifts?

Otto Scharmer writes in "Theory U" (op. cit.):

> What I see rising is a new form of presence and power that starts to spontaneously grow from and through small groups and networks of people. It's a different quality of connection, a different way of being present with one another and with what wants to emerge. When groups begin to operate from a real future possibility, they start to tap into a different social field from what they normally experience. It manifests through a shift in the quality of thinking, conversing and collective action. When that shift happens, people can connect with a deeper source of creativity and knowing and move beyond the patterns of the past.

This is how new political systems can emerge—when small groups or sometimes also large networks tap into a different quality of connection with themselves, each other, and the future. So far, I've been part of such a process once in my life, at the first assembly of the group that would found NEOS, and at the assemblies that followed.

Political entrepreneurs have to know the past, to avoid repeating its mistakes. But they have to lead from the future to help it emerge, precisely because the present is so powerful. The "morbid symptoms" in the interregnum we are experiencing are powerful distractions. Rather than fighting them, political entrepreneurs should focus on building a new system so our societies can leave the interregnum. Muddling through will not do. To have the required transform-ability, they have to be in touch with and look after themselves—after all, as former CEO of Hanover Insurance Bill O'Brien told Otto Scharmer: "the success of an intervention depends on the *interior condition* of the intervenor" (my emphasis),

3.6   Leading Political Entrepreneurs

Entrepreneurs, be it in business, the social sector or politics, are difficult. It is in their nature to question assumptions, challenge the status quo and have little respect for authority. That applies to anything and everything. So, leading them can be a pain.

Entrepreneurial leadership, therefore, is essential when leading entrepreneurs. For this, order is just as important as autonomy and freedom to act. The precise balance varies according to organisational phase and cultural context. The whole idea of entrepreneurial leadership is *empowering other entrepreneurs*—in the case of political enterprises, other political entrepreneurs, at all levels.

"To build up local and regional organisations is crucial, but those people have to be obligated to act in the common interest, via function, or at least via moral pressure" Beate Meinl-Reisinger, at the time Chairwoman of NEOS Vienna and later Chairwoman and Group Leader of NEOS, told me. "At the same time, if you want people to act, you need to give them power. And that can only work if you design the organisation as a kind of hybrid—one that has hierarchies on the one side, but at the same time is operating in a network logic. That allows decentralised units that have the power to act. Without parameters it doesn't work, but having too many parameters makes people frustrated, particularly if they are volunteers. In a volunteer-based organisation, everyone has their particular interests and things they like, and they should be able to pursue them, whatever they may be."

En Marche has understood this. In the first phase, every member could establish a "local committee" via a common digital platform, without any bureaucracy. They were empowered to organise events and feedback, again via a digital type-form. This feedback was used for Macron's speeches, and for the En Marche policy platform. Currently, En Marche experiments with new digital formats like Microlearning and a MOOC (Massive Open Online Course). Microlearning is an e-learning format that breaks up larger chunks of information into small learning units and short-term learning activities, so that members can learn new things and skills without investing a large amount of time. A MOOC is an online course that allows an unlimited number of people to enrol on pre-designed curricula via their PCs or mobile phones, independent of time and location. This way, En Marche can train their members and activists almost in parallel, on a nation-wide level.

Political entrepreneurs often have no previous background in party politics, or any cross-over from business, the public sector or civil society. To understand the different logics, it is helpful to have people leading them with experience in all those fields. Nick Lovegrove and Matthew Thomas call such leaders "triple-strength" ("Triple-Strength Leadership", *Harvard Business Review*, 2013).

3.7 In Times of Crisis

Leadership makes the most difference in times of crisis. Political start-ups that travel without the baggage of traditional parties can use that to their advantage. They can become "projection screens" for the new, for better or for worse.

The right-wing national conservative Law and Justice party (PiS) in Poland, itself only founded in 2001, won the parliamentary elections on October 25, 2015 with almost 38%. Six months earlier, their candidate Andrzej Duda had won the Presidency. The previously governing centrist Civic Platform was in tatters.

The liberal political start-up Nowoczesna, which had just entered parliament for the first time with 7.6% of the vote, became the primary target of PiS attacks. Amazingly, however, Nowoczesna's new parliamentarians were not only able to withstand the political aggression of the government, they also did a great job of fighting back in public. This led to a steep climb in the polls, which saw them eclipse even PiS in some polls by the end of 2015. They became the effective leader of the opposition, with an approval of around 20% from early 2016 to the beginning of 2017.

At the end of 2016 Nowoczesna found that a track record doesn't only bring baggage. It also brings a more stable voter base. Poland faced a constitutional crisis. PiS moved to appoint its own nominees to serve as judges on the constitutional tribunal, Poland's Supreme Court. The opposition cried foul. There were anti-government demonstrations jointly organised by the opposition parties, but the government did not budge. The crisis continued into the Christmas break. The opposition did not budge either, and sustained its protests with sit-in strikes in the hall of Parliament.

During the protests, Ryszard Petru and his colleague Joanna Schmidt went on a personal trip to Portugal. The PiS government claimed in the state media that Petru, one of the most vocal members in opposition, had decided to leave the country while his colleagues were occupying Parliament. They provided photos. This didn't go down well with the public. From February, 2017, Nowoczesna went into almost free fall in the polls, hitting bottom with 5% in Summer, 2017. In November, 2017, Petru lost the Presidency of Nowoczesna to Katarzyna Lubnauer (see Chap. 10). This was another first for Poland—never before had a party leadership changed hands in a democratic vote.

3.8 Leading to Transform

A transformational political leader, according to Archie Brown, is "one who plays a decisive role in introducing *systemic change*, whether of the political or economic system of his or her country. . ." (op. cit.). Brown sees Charles de Gaulle in France, Adolfo Suarez in Spain, and Mikhail Gorbachev in the Soviet Union as members of this exclusive group.

Transformational leaders aim not just for incremental, but for systemic change, but they're not revolutionary leaders. To bring about the new order, revolutionary leaders raze whole the system to the ground. That's the leadership of Lenin, and of modern-day revolutionaries, such as US President Donald Trump's former advisor Steve Bannon. "Lenin," Bannon once proclaimed in an interview, "wanted to destroy the state, and that's my goal too. I want to bring everything crashing down, and destroy all of today's establishment" ("Steve Bannon, Trump's Top Guy, Told me he was a 'Leninist'", Roland Radosh, *The Daily Beast*, August 22, 2016). Revolutionary leadership is deeply destructive. Transformational leadership is constructive. It wants to, to help the system evolve, while preserving the good in its current form.

To achieve such system transform-ability, political entrepreneurs must transform themselves first. Ronan Harrington, founder of Alter Ego, which explores the future of progressive liberal politics, made much of this point in a structured question and answer session with me in a hotel in Berlin, in August 2017.

Towards a more open, authentic and vulnerable politics: A conversation with Ronan Harrington

JL: How would you frame the problem that progressive liberal politics is facing, and that political entrepreneurs need to address?

RH: On the individual level, progressive politicians are not operating at enough emotional and spiritual depth. There is a generation of liberal politicians who are hyper-rational, scripted, aloof. There is a hunger for more authenticity and honesty in politics. People need to feel liberal political leaders the way they feel Trump.

But this visceral quality has so far been exploited by the far right. We have to out-depth the far right and get to the emotions below the emotions. We have to work through regression to get to progress.

JL: What can platforms like Alter Ego contribute to addressing this problem?

RH: A space for centrist politicians to be open, authentic and vulnerable with each other, to do inner work and leadership development. A space where they practice greater depth. Political Entrepreneurship is not transformative until it has been transformed. The transformers first have to transform themselves. They need to model vulnerability.

We are stuck in a dualistic, polarised political culture. We are failing to see that centre-left and centre-right are in a dialectical process. Speaking in leadership development terms, we need to move to second-tier thinking, beyond this duality. The state would not be there without the market, and vice versa. A renewed centre is a centre than can hold both the centre-left and the centre-right.

We need to be able to hold that greater complexity, without falling into relativism. That requires practice, and places to practice: how do you hold perspectives? It is not just an intellectual exercise, it is a deeply emotional one. This requires a space where politicians can have a human connection.

JL: How do you see the relation between individual psychological development and systemic progress?

RH: On an individual level, needs must be met before progress can happen. There is a need for spaces that profile the importance of psychological development, and take it out of the private domain, into our institutions. The crisis we are facing is a crisis of human capacity. Cultural development also needs to be put on the agenda. Politics needs to move beyond traditionally implementing policies, and foster a culture that can survive and flourish in the world we are living in.

Deeper change often comes from grassroots activities, from the political fringes. Often they are disconnected from mainstream institutions. There needs to be spaces to make those relationships happen.

(continued)

JL: What challenges do you see liberalism itself facing?

RH: We need to have uncomfortable conversations about the blind spots of liberalism. What is the shadow of liberalism? Because it is universal, there is a failure to appreciate what I would call a "compatriot partiality"—feeling stronger solidarity with one's own. There is condescension towards people exercising it, and there are feelings of superiority and misanthropy towards them.

In the US, for example, there is unprocessed hate of the "stupid people who voted for Trump". As long as progressive politics smells of that, it will not form a full relationship with these communities. It is not enough to say we need to go there. The Right have way more respect for their voters, are less aloof, and they are in the communities.

But it is tough. There needs to be spaces for greater authenticity and vulnerability, to encourage people to step into the arena. There is so much transformation needed of the liberal progressive persona and its mind-set, before any transformation on the political system can happen.

Political entrepreneurs need to first understand themselves, before they can develop a deep understanding of the political system around them. How they arrive at that kind of understanding is the focus of the next chapter.

For the reader who wants to follow the journey of the political entrepreneurs in a more visual way, the roadmap to political transformation, which gives a summary of all stages and key tasks from here on, can be found in the appendix.

Understanding Political Systems

4

Matthias Strolz introduces his book "Why we don't trust politicians—and what they (would) have to do to change that" ("Warum wir Politikern nicht trauen: und was sie tun müss(t)en, damit sich das ändert", Kremayr & Scheriau, 2011) with these three words: "I love politics!"

To understand a system thoroughly, you need to acquire an intimacy with it that's comparable to love. And you must be ready to suffer for your love. The German word "Leidenschaft" and the English word "passion" are antonyms of "Verstand"/ "reason". They also share the ambivalence of a driving force that promises pleasure as much as pain—painful pleasure as much as pleasurable pain. If that sounds masochistic, it is because it is.

All political entrepreneurs are passionate political animals in one way or another, each and every one a *zoon politikon*—an intensely social and political being. Which is why, prior to entering mainstream politics, they can often be found on the political periphery.

Political entrepreneurs may have been consultants, advisors, academics, NGO staff, activists, journalists, public intellectuals—or in the corridors of power, studying the decision-makers, and learning from their triumphs and failures. They may even have been decision-makers themselves, before they fell out with the system that put them in decision-making positions.

In fact, that was the norm for liberal and centrist political start-ups in the past: a Member of Parliament (MP), or sometimes a group of MPs, decide to break with their party, and found a new party; a parliamentary inside job. They were, so to speak, "entrepreneurial politicians", rather than political entrepreneurs.

Increasingly however, as I show in this book, previously non-political entrepreneurs and entrepreneurially minded citizens are now daring to enter the political arena.

Take Progressive Slovakia, which was founded by a group of ten entrepreneurs and activists, and aims to provide "progressive solutions to social problems". According to Martin Dubéci, a public policy advisor who I interviewed in Vienna

© Springer Nature Switzerland AG 2019
J. Lentsch, *Political Entrepreneurship*,
https://doi.org/10.1007/978-3-030-02861-9_4

in October 2017, they felt Slovak politics was stuck. They wanted to create a new policy platform, with new values—something that cut through the old orthodoxies, between right and left politics, and was also new in terms of how political organisations were constructed.

Or take NEOS, which was started by an entrepreneur and a business executive. Both had long been on Austria's political periphery, and both had long been dissatisfied with the current political system. It is this mix of entrepreneurial politicos and political entrepreneurs that is so powerful. These people bring a new mind-set as well as a new skill-set to politics. Perhaps most importantly, they are personally and professionally grounded in the real world, instead of having been captured by the political system at critical stages of their lives.

Political entrepreneurs do not fall from the skies. Even if they had not been active in politics before, it takes them years, even decades of studying, to develop a deep understanding of the political system. They may not have realised it, but they were engaged in "implicit learning" about politics. Often, you will find they were running for student councils at school or university. In addition to providing an early education in political structures and processes, that also forges bonds: many of the core group of 40 citizens that founded NEOS in 2012 had known each other from student councils in the 1990s.

They may have been involved in youth organisations, sports clubs, church groups or associations. Already then, knowingly or not, they may have been amassing what Robert Putnam calls "Social Capital" ("Bowling Alone", Simon and Schuster, 2000): relationships and often weak social ties with peers, colleagues and mentors that they subsequently cultivate, and use at a later stage of their lives.

They were ready to take on responsibility, and found joy in serving a good cause as much as in exercising power. "I was in politics in my youth—I was the President of the Young Democratic Left, as it was called", Ivan Stefunko, a co-founder of the Slovak political start-up Progrésivne, told me during our Skype interview in April, 2018. "It was the Youth Movement of Social Democracy in Slovakia, before it became SMER (a social democratic party). I've also been very active in the international sphere; I've gone to every social democratic youth or progressive event in Europe and the world." Like other political entrepreneurs, he got fed up with politics in his youth, and left the arena before getting involved with the politics of the grown-ups. In 2002, when he saw what was happening with the Social Democratic party and the democratic Left in Slovakia, he resigned from party politics, only to return to it 14 years later.

Political entrepreneurs may have been avid readers early on: "I experienced my childhood with books, somewhat detached from the world. . ... I lived largely on texts and words. . ... The secret, intimate education through books was stronger than it appeared, and gave the world a depth you do not encounter easily," Emmanuel Macron wrote in his book "Revolution" in 2016.

Or they may have taken a particular interest in their immediate political world and what drove it: "Already in my youth I was a keen collector of media reports about the occurrences in my home valley", Matthias Strolz wrote.

They may even have expected early on that they would be in politics at some point in their lives: "That I would be in politics—this purpose, which I really see as a calling—that was clear relatively early. With hindsight, I'd say that started in school. In which form, though, I did not know," Strolz told me.

Finally, just like all entrepreneurs, political entrepreneurs learn by doing. They learn continuously from trial and error. Returning to the beginning of this chapter, to understand deeply is to love, and to *do*.

"You can study politics, but you have to experience it at some point to understand it, and its links to systemics, group dynamics, sociology, macro- and microeconomics and psychology", said Strolz.

Sometimes this type of understanding is catalysed by a life event. Yair Lapid, who later became the founder of the Israeli centrist political start-up Yesh Atid, had been anchor-man of Israel's largest news show. As a journalist, he had been around politics half his life. But then his father, who had also been a journalist, fell ill.

"There was a moment I was in the Ichilov hospital in Tel Aviv," he told me during our interview at the ALDE [the Alliance of Liberals and Democrats for Europe] Congress in Amsterdam in December, 2017. "My father was in the last week of his life and we were watching a basketball game together. He told me 'You are gonna see the next game by yourself'. And the next game was the week after, meaning he was not going to be alive in the coming week. So we stayed up all night and discussed this, and he said 'I am not only leaving you and the family, but also a country'. Not in a Louis XIV kind of way, but in an emotional kind of way."

He paused, and looked deeply into my eyes. "My father was a Holocaust survivor. I was raised to understand that Israel is not only a country but is also a safe haven for Jews, the answer to anti-Semitism and a very, very personal matter. So that moment gave rise to my political career and my constant awareness of the fact that, contrary to what we think, countries can't exist by themselves. They need people who are willing to dedicate their lives to them."

He emphasised that it took some time for him to process what had been sparked inside of him at that moment. But then things went quickly. "One day I couldn't do it. . . I couldn't stand on the side-lines anymore. . . I remember there was a night I was sitting with my wife and my eldest son. My other son was playing on the PlayStation in his room. And I said 'You know what, it's Friday night. On Sunday, I am going to announce that I am leaving television, and I am going to enter politics to establish a new party.'"

Lapid met a former Prime Minister, who asked him if he was crazy, and advised him to join one of the existing parties. Lapid countered that the existing parties, and what they represented, were exactly the reason why he wanted to establish a new one. That Sunday he gave a press conference, and announced he would leave television, to form a political party. He laughed: "I don't know whether the rest is history, but it's my history."

4.1   Envisioning a New Politics

How does a new politics *feel*? "I was put directly into the field", Aziz François Ndiaye told me during my visit in November 2017 to the En Marche headquarters at Rue Sainte-Anne in Paris' second arrondissement. On the right bank of the Seine in an up-and-coming district, the building looked more like a co-working space than the office of a political party. In the lobby, a group of young people sat at a table with their laptops and mobiles: their job was to respond to the thousands of citizen enquiries reaching En Marche after their victory in June.

Nowadays, Aziz is in charge of field operations at En Marche. In 2016, he was a former entrepreneur who was ready to leave France. But he gave it a try, sent in his application, was recruited, and from then on, has never looked back. "Actually, the first thing we did was work on the programme of La Grande Marche. Organising the teams, talking to citizens and having them tell us exactly what they were expecting from the country. I was directly involved in this process, and given the responsibility of organising teams in the field. I was totally free to organise the work. That was very new for me. Of course we had guidelines and the programme and the strategy. But to this day one of our peculiarities is to give total responsibility to our 'representants' (departmental representatives), so they organise themselves on the field. This is very important. And this is probably one of the keys to our success."

But how do you arrive at such a new approach? Once you have a deep understanding of the current political system, how do you construct a vision of a new one?

One answer that emerged from the various interviews I conducted over the course of 12 months was: start writing.

4.2   The Power of the Pen

In France, it is a long-standing tradition that aspiring political leaders formulate their political ideas in books ahead of elections. Often, they come in the form of emotional pamphlets. Accordingly, Emmanuel Macron published his book "Revolution" in 2016. On the first page, he wrote that it was impossible to react to the major changes of our time with "the same people and ideas, and to believe we can put the wheel of history into reverse" (Xo Editions, 2016). "If we face up to the reality of our world, we can gain hope once again." He wrote about those who think France is in decline, and those who think France can continue as is—and that they are both wrong. "It's not the country that has failed, but its models and recipes." He then itemised the main challenges and opportunities of our era—"globalisation, digitalisation, growing inequality, climate change, worldwide conflicts and terrorism, the crumbling of Europe, the crisis of democracy and Western societies, the doubts at the heart of our society".

On subsequent pages he outlined what he called "a democratic revolution", and the movement he was about to build, by inviting his fellow citizens to become engaged. He reflected critically on the current state of globalisation, the need for internationally effective measures and a "common morale". He criticised the generational injustice of ever-higher public debt, and pledged to reduce public expenditure. He wanted to transform the French "catch-up economy" into a genuinely innovative economy, by re-industrialising the nation. To achieve that, he saw the need to invest in human capital, through education in particular, in digital infrastructure, and in ecological change. "The economic and the ecological imperatives are not opposites, they will complement each other ever more in the future." He wanted to adapt bureaucracy and over-regulation, such as the French labour law, to the needs of the twenty-first century. Tax law, on the other hand, should "reward the ones willing to take a risk." The "most noble task of politics", Macron concluded, "is to change reality, to become active and give power to those who act."

This became his overarching message: he wanted to do politics differently. "A talent for speaking differently, rather than for arguing well is the chief instrument of cultural change," wrote the American philosopher Richard Rorty in "Contingency, irony and solidarity" (Cambridge University Press, 1989). Macron certainly spoke differently in his speeches, and through his book.

"I write books to sort myself out intellectually", NEOS Chairman Matthias Strolz told me while we were having lunch in a restaurant between the Parliament building and the NEOSphere, the open plan headquarter of NEOS in Vienna. "Putting my thoughts between two book covers, and structuring them in this way, leads to order. Order is important to me to be at full strength."

So far, he has written four books, two before co-founding the citizen movement he later led into Parliament. One, "Why We Don't Trust Politicians, and what they (would) have to do to change that" (op. cit), he regards, with hindsight, as "an instructional manual that I wrote for myself. Today I see that book as the script for the founding of a party."

Strolz said that while writing the book, "I felt a lot of 'Angstlust' (anxiety-desire) that translated itself into confusion". This internal conflict, and the related ambivalence, was a recurrent theme in my interviews with political entrepreneurs, and a regular accompaniment of phases such as letting go of the old, and letting come the new. At the same time, several of them told me that it can also take up too much mental bandwidth and stand in the way of development. It highlights that developing a vision involves getting ready—emotionally, personally and professionally.

Many ideas Strolz outlined in "Why We Don't Trust Politicians", about a more authentic, open, participative and entrepreneurial politics, were realised with NEOS 2 years later. But he himself did not realise that would happen at the time, because "I personally, at that stage of my life, was not yet ready." As I will argue in the pages that follow, Political Entrepreneurship is very much about the right timing, expressed in the Greek concept of *Kairos*.

Ryszard Petru, the founder of Nowoczesna, wrote several books, including two children's books on economics. In January 2015, 9 months before the Polish parliamentary elections, he published a book called "The end of the free market? The origins of the crisis" ("Koniec wolnego rynku? Geneza kryzysu", with Łukasz Lipiński, NCK, 2014) in which he argued that it was damaging state interventions, rather than the free market, that led to the global crisis of 2008, and set out many ideas that would re-appear later in the Nowoczesna manifesto.

If writing a book seems like a tall order, here is a tip: to warm up one's muscles for such an intellectual climb over months or even years, start reading books. Lots of them. Political leaders are readers. Or, at least, they were. You may not have the time for it once you enter the political arena, so it is all the more important to take the time *before* you do it. Time and time again my interview partners mentioned to me important books they read at critical stages, or described how they had a relevant idea while reading about someone else's ideas.

Sometimes, however, it is a shorter form of writing that kicks off a new political movement, the manifesto, the main political marketing document since the dawn of democracy. It's still in use today.

Ciudadanos was founded in Catalonia In Spain as "Ciutadans" (Catalan for "Citizens") in 2006 with a manifesto. It was written by 15 well-known intellectuals, journalists and lawyers, and subsequently published in the media.

Nine years later, when Ciudadanos moved onto the national stage, they presented their main ideas of a new politics in the form of a short manifesto that was widely circulated among the public. The ideas were then written up in a book ("Recuperar el future", Península, 2015) authored by Luis Garicano, a London School of Economics professor, and Toni Roldán Monés, Ciudadanos's Director of Programme. When I visited the offices of the Ciudadanos parliamentary group in Madrid in June, 2017, Roldán Monés, a dark-haired, soft spoken, highly determined 35 year-old Catalan economist, told me "we knew there are three crucial problems in Spain. So we basically had three main policy pillars. We had a huge problem in the labour market. We had a huge problem in the institutions, in terms of crony capitalism. And we had a huge problem in education. So on the basis of these three axes, we drafted a number of policies, and tried to make them as sexy as possible."

Intermediate forms, between a brief manifesto and a full book, have also proved effective.

Progressive Slovakia, for example, published a 140-page (described as "ridiculously long" by Board member, Martin Dubéci) policy document. "So we have put this effort in to defining the centre ground", Dubéci told me during his visit to NEOS Lab in November, 2017, "because it sometimes gets really confusing when people ask like 'oh, they are centrist. What's centrist? Is it like the arithmetic middle between the left and right? Or is it something that has its unique qualities?'"

Dubéci reminded me that they also put an essay online entitled "Move On", in which they said: "The most important question of Slovak politics is not about the Left or the Right, but about the tension between progressive and reactionary powers... We are convinced that the priorities we strive for can be agreed on by a progressive Christian or liberal, a sensible right-winger or a socialist... In principle, we can all agree on the main issues within education, healthcare, and poverty, especially among the Roma community. Now we need determination and the skills to change things" (https://www.progresivne.sk/en/move-on/).

Yair Lapid, the Chairperson of Israeli political start-up Yesh Atid, published an essay entitled "The Return of the Center", to describe his notion of a new centrist politics. In it, he refers to the Austrian-born philosopher Martin Buber's social vision of the state as a commonwealth of communities. "If we go about it in the proper way, with the proper forms of cooperation", Lapid wrote, "we will see in the coming years more and more centrist parties winning, leading nations, taking the reins in a world that seems to have shirked the obligation of responsibility." To him, centrist politics is not the midpoint between Left and Right—it is "the equilibrium against which Right and Left define themselves", and which is about "even-handed moderation". It offers, Lapid argues, "The Best of all Worlds": patriotism and a pro-economy attitude that revolved around the employment of the working person, but also pro human rights and a progressive outlook towards the future.

The first manifesto of Yesh Atid, Yair Lapid drafted by himself, working late at night while his children slept. He then put it on Facebook, opening it up for comments by the crowd. "And people had comments" he recalled when I spoke to him at the ALDE congress in Amsterdam in November 2017. "We discussed the comments. And people came in and wrote things like 'you know, this is a very good summary, but you don't know what you are talking when you talk about housing' and I said 'Okay, I never said we had the entire cerebrum in one place, come on board, help us!' It was like open source. It wasn't like a platform for me to present to the people and tell them 'this is it'. And then I wrote the second version, with all the remarks and ideas people had. . . you do it in good faith and you are willing to admit mistakes; that is the most important thing."

Writing blogs on Facebook or elsewhere, cultivating an online community, and constantly incorporating feedback as Lapid did, is a great way to collaborate and mobilise. It is also excellent practice for writing a book. Blogs are a great format to structure one or two central political thoughts within a couple of hours. If writing a book is a marathon, blogs are like sprints. They do not need to be as thoroughly researched and edited as a book. Also, they are an excellent way to run rapid feedback loops, and get quick responses to ideas. If you want to change anything, you can do so with a click.

Publishing the blogs or political comments of others can also be useful. This is what Ivan Stefunko, the founder of Progrésivne (Progressive Slovakia) did. After he left politics in 2002, disappointed by the democratic left, he started to publish a political weekly. This was also how he started out as an entrepreneur: "Because we had to finance the paper, I had to learn how to be an entrepreneur" he told me on Skype in April, 2018. "It was quite difficult to survive."

While doing this, he started another entrepreneurial venture, the Slovak version of Euractiv.com, an independent pan-European media network specialising in EU policies.

"I started Euractiv.sk [Slovak], and then with a partner and others, Euractiv.cz [Czech], .hu [hungarian] and .pl [Polish]. I co-founded the majority of the national versions of Euractiv. And then I became the Network Director of Euractiv.com. So I became quite active on the internet, and then I founded several internet companies in Slovakia and the region, such as Pelikan, the biggest seller of airline tickets in Slovakia and the region, which turns over about €80 million a year."

It did not stop there: over the past 15 years, Stefunko has founded, co-founded or invested in more than 50 companies.

4.3   Discussion and Debate

Another way to encourage ideas that lead to a vision of new politics to emerge, is to join forces with like-minded people, and harvest their creativity in a structured process. The MIT-based action researcher Otto Scharmer calls this "co-sensing"; a group process he describes as "observe, observe, observe, and going to the places of most potential and listening with your mind and heart wide open" (op. cit.).

In 2007, I helped Matthias Strolz organise a conference in Linz, in Austria. The main question we formulated was: "What should a new style and new forms of debate look like in Austrian politics?" As we wanted to walk the talk, we based the day on the Open Space-method for large groups, which allows for self-organisation and co-creation by the participants. Our claim was that "we want a new style in the political debate: to approach each other, listen to each other, be open for critical discourse, be open for critique, and have the courage to tell the truth." If all things went well, perhaps the day would even give birth to a new political movement.

The objective was to gather 150 people. There was a participation fee of €25. As this did not cover the costs, some organisations also co-funded the event. In terms of participants, the objective was met. There were also lots of good ideas. However, the hope that the occasion would also kick-start a new movement was not realised. Why? In hindsight, "too little focus, too little homogeneity of the participants, too little tightness of the design" according to Strolz. The event was a one-off, and like many political initiatives, it fizzled out. In the end, it left many even more frustrated than before. Perhaps it was simply that we were not ready at the time. Remember Bill O'Brien's observation that the success of an intervention depends on the inner state of the intervenor (see Chap. 3.5). It took another 6 years for the next, and this time successful, shot.

Sometimes, words are not enough. It may take an even deeper, personal dive to unlock the vision required to break old patterns, un-think the present, and help the political future to emerge. A change in the processing mode may be required, from the intellectual to the holistic.

Matthias Strolz, for example, went on a 5 day and four night long "vision quest" in the Viennese woods, which he wrote about in his book "Die vierte Kränkung" ("The fourth slight"), which he co-authored with Barbara Guwak (Goldegg Gesellschaft, 2012). There, he told me during our interview in November 2017, he gained the insight to "be vigilant, be awake. Decide." The successful entrepreneur realised he was "a gardener of life. I cultivate social fields". He sees himself this way to this day. "I am not a politician—I am *also* a politician—as a gardener of life. I am a political entrepreneur, and an entrepreneur." Although he did not anticipate he would found a party less than a couple of years later, this deep experience became central to his transform-ability—the ability not only fundamentally to re-think the political system, but also to have an impact on it.

There are various routes to imagining a new politics, some more intellectual, like writing, some more action-based, like large-group workshops, and some more experiential. All have their merit. For political entrepreneurs, however, it may take years to distil the deep thoughts that don't just scratch the surface of the political system, but aim at its very heart.

Building Models for Political Change

5

> *If someone asked me, what the most important aspect in the*
> *build-up of a political start-up is, I would say it is how you lay*
> *the foundations. Just like with a house. From that already you*
> *can see whether it will survive in the long term, or not.*
>
> Feri Thierry (in conversation, April 2018)

Beginnings matter. While they do not determine the outcome altogether, they shape it. Path dependency, the idea that decisions you will make in the future are limited by decisions you make right now, is strong in politics. History matters, and the organisational history of a political enterprise, enshrined in its "organisational DNA", has consequences for its growth potential and its resilience. This organisational history is written not only via formal decisions, but also through the countless informal exchanges on all levels. This history starts long before the day of intellectual conception.

Building a political enterprise to its successful entry into the national Parliament can take as long as 10 years as with Ciudadanos, or as short as 4 months as with Nowoczesna (and, depending on how you calculate, even less time for En Marche). There is no right or wrong timeframe, and if you look for the one ideal template, you will not find it in politics. What you face instead is a plethora of trade-offs and hard choices that all come with costs and benefits attached.

In the following pages I outline each building phase step-by-step. Depending on your initial position and your resources, you might be able to take the short route and bypass some of the phases. The roadmap is based on the long route of a political start-up that starts from scratch, with no resources whatsoever. A graphic summary of the roadmap is included in an appendix at the end of this book.

© Springer Nature Switzerland AG 2019
J. Lentsch, *Political Entrepreneurship*,
https://doi.org/10.1007/978-3-030-02861-9_5

5.1   Prepare

As with many words in the Political Entrepreneurship lexicon, "prepare" has two meanings: preparing for the start-up, and preparing yourself, and your immediate environment. You need to get ready for what is to come.

Preparation often only looks like preparation in retrospect. It is a process that may take years. Political start-ups do not appear out of thin air. Preparation often takes place in parallel—people prepare political start-ups while they are busy doing other stuff. For a good reason: As Eric Ries shows in "The Start-up Way" (Currency, 2017), somewhat counter-intuitively, business entrepreneurs who quit their jobs early on to work on their new start-up are on average less successful than those who stay in their jobs longer. There has been no similar research to date on political entrepreneurs, but I would say, based on my interviews, that this applies to them too.

Depending on the context, even the later stages of preparation will often take place below the radar, either deliberately, to avoid attracting the attention of potential opponents at a time when the start-up project is still highly vulnerable, or simply because of a lack of access to the required resources.

Politics is about collective action. Therefore, preparing a political start-up has a lot to do with cultivating relationships, on the individual and the organisational level.

5.1.1   Individual Level

On the individual level, there are a few key roles to fill. They may be informal, but they are certainly crucial. In no particular order these essential roles are:

- sparring partners
- mentors
- accomplices
- professional advisors
- matrons/patrons
- first followers

Sparring Partners
As already noted (see Sect. 1.6) "sparring partners" are trusted peers with whom one has serious but friendly arguments. They may not be the closest of friends, they may have differing interests, they may even be competitors to some extent. And there may come a time to part ways with them. But what they have to offer can be very valuable, particularly in the early stages of preparation: sound judgment, relevant experiences and realistic perspectives. They are not afraid to point out the blind spots of the political entrepreneur, and to pour cold water on wishful thinking. In the early stages of preparation, they are an important resource for vetting ideas, avoiding dead-ends and staying on the right track. They might never get involved in a deeper way with the start-up, but they do not leak information, and they respect the personal relationship.

Ivan Stefunko, a co-founder of Progrésivne (Progressive Slovakia), told me during our Skype interview in April, 2018, that before he and the small group around him started to think about the possibility of creating a political party, they created a non-governmental organisation (NGO) called "Slovak Alliance for an Innovative Economy"—a group of entrepreneurs to spar with them on a regular basis. "We were 30–40 people, and initially started to discuss economics." But after several debates, they came to the conclusion that they had to change the society and politics in their country as a whole—"education, regional disparities, and so on. As entrepreneurs we started to discuss politics and policies much more than the entrepreneurial environment." Thus, the NGO, and the group organised with it, became the incubator for the subsequent start-up.

Mentors
Mentors are people with more life and professional experience than the political entrepreneur. They may have sympathies with the political entrepreneur personally and also with the cause, but they are often detached from and disinterested in the project, as such. Both their experience and disinterest allow them to hold a mirror up to the political entrepreneur, and give wise counsel and guidance. They can also be important reality checkers, if they themselves have been politically active. They may also be able to open a few important doors that would otherwise have been closed to the political entrepreneur.

For Matthias Strolz of NEOS, one of those mentors was Erhard Busek, the former Chairman of the conservative Österreichische Volkspartei (ÖVP). Even though Busek remained with the ÖVP, he sponsored Strolz personally, and helped him to expand his network over the years.

Accomplices
Accomplices are partners-in-crime who are ready to go all-in, and become co-founders of the political start-up. They believe in the project, and the political entrepreneur, when no one else does. Needless to say, a trusting relationship and personal chemistry are just as important as professional fit for this role.

On October 10, 2011, the online platform of the Austrian daily "Der Standard" published a double interview by Lukas Kapeller and Rainer Schüller, with the then State Secretary Josef Ostermayer of the Social Democrats and the then independent political advisor Matthias Strolz. A few months earlier, Strolz had published his book "Why We Don't Trust Politicians" (op. cit.). The interview focused on the state of Austrian politics, its relationship with the media and what had gone wrong, or right, in the Republic. The interview culminated in the following exchange:

derStandard.at	Would you advise Mr. Strolz to go into politics?
Ostermayer	I am not sure he wants to put himself through this. After all, he writes that politicians act as lightning rods for daily

(continued)

	frustrations, like when somebody got into an argument with his partner, or you just missed the tram. I believe he does not want to be the lightning rod, but prefers to write about lightning rods.
derStandard.at	Mr. Strolz?
Strolz	I will be in politics. That I know from the depth of my being. But it is not yet the right time. You must sense the right time, and you must be willing to wait.

The next day, Strolz received a call from Veit Dengler. The two had met 4 years earlier, at a day-long Open Space-event on New Politics in Linz, Austria. Subsequently, they got to know each other better through the so called "Eulennest" (Owl's Nest) group, named after a Viennese wine bar where a small group of politically interested friends and acquaintances regularly met to spar with each other, and to dissect the latest political rumours.

Dengler, a graduate of Harvard Kennedy School, was General Manager of the IT company, Dell, in Bratislava at the time. He had a successful international business career, and would later go on to become the CEO of the Swiss Neue Zürcher Zeitung media group and a director of the global Bauer Media Group. But he had always taken a keen interest in politics, particularly in his native Austria. Back in 2008, he had even offered to take unpaid leave to run the conservative ÖVP's election campaign. But, as was the experience of so many political entrepreneurs, the structures of such a traditional party were not up to taking on and incorporating energy from the outside. He declined an invitation to join ÖVP's "Personality Committee", which was merely symbolic, and without any impact.

"The call from Veit lasted perhaps 30 seconds" Strolz recalled. "He said: 'The time is right *now*, isn't it?' And I said: 'Yes, the time is right'. And then we said: 'Ok, let's do it.' It was Kairos as only Kairos can".

He realised that "I was all-in at that point. The decision had been taken, there is no going back. With everything I am and have, I am putting myself into service."

In November, Dengler and Strolz met with Feri Thierry, a long-time friend and colleague of Strolz who ran his own Public Relations company, and who had previously been involved with the "Platform for Open Politics", a civil society organisation on the periphery of the conservative ÖVP that advocated a more liberal politics in Austria (see his quote at the beginning of this Chapter). The three became accomplices, and started to form a new political movement. They got out their virtual rolodexes, and began to compile an invitation list.

The first assembly was convened 4 months later, in February 2012, under the codename "Phoenix Austria".

Ivan Stefunko of Progressive Slovakia had become disillusioned, and left the political arena in 2002. Well, almost, as he told me during our Skype interview in

April 2018. During the subsequent 16 years, he kept in touch with policy makers and people from civil society.

"A very good friend of mine, Martin Filko, was the Chief Economist of Slovakia, at the Ministry of Finance" Stefunko told me. "He was the head of the Institute for Financial Policy. He was a very influential state bureaucrat. He wrote articles, and was invited to many public events. He was very influential, despite his youth." Filko was just around 30 at the time. "He was a child prodigy, as they say."

The same problems Ivan saw from the private business perspective, Martin saw from a state perspective. The Slovak state was not entrepreneurial enough; it was averse to change and to new kinds of communication with its citizens. They kept exchanging their views for 6 years. That was how they became accomplices.

In 2016, Filko decided it was time to leave the civil service and create a new kind of think-tank, to promote his ideas. When Filko told Stefunko of his plans, his friend said: "Martin, don't you want to merge our worlds and our surroundings? The state employees who work for you, share the same vision of a modern Slovakia, and I have like-minded entrepreneur friends, people from the NGO sphere, and journalists... don't you want to do something together? We are going to fund and promote your think tank." They started to plan for a think-tank that would press for a modern, economically progressive, and socially and environmentally responsible Slovakia, which had the potential to evolve into a political start-up.

"I introduced Martin to a lot of influential people from my world, and he did the same from his side. But the day after we decided we were going to start a very formal think-tank, with the ability to evolve into a political party, he died. He drowned in the Danube. If it had been a movie, people would say 'what a shitty ending!' It was tragic."

I talked to Stefunko on Skype 2 years and a week after Filko's death. His voice still shook when he talked about it. His friend, accomplice and confidant was dead. It was the end. But it was also a beginning. "We stopped working on the project after the funeral, but 3 weeks later, people I and Martin had approached started to say 'nobody can replace Martin. But on the other hand, let's work with the message he has left for us.'" About a year later, Progrésivne was born.

Professional Advisors

Professional advisors have particular domain expertise that is critical to the political start-up's success, and that the political entrepreneur and his or her accomplices do not have. They may sympathise with the project and/or the entrepreneur and be ready to offer their expertise, particularly at the beginning.

Furthermore, on the European level, political start-ups can tap into the expertise of traditional parties and their networks. For example, the Alliance of Liberals and Democrats for Europe (ALDE), the European political party, has many excellent advisors in various fields, from campaigning to data analysis. By working with them, political start-ups can make use of existing knowledge, and do not have to re-invent the wheel.

Matrons/Patrons

Matrons and patrons are acquaintances in high places who are ready to contribute critical resources—their high-calibre networks, funding, infrastructure, or access to broadcasting—to the political start-up. If they are ready to go public as supporters, they lend their public credibility to the political entrepreneur, and give the project as well as the political entrepreneur more gravitas.

One of NEOS's patrons has been Hans-Peter Haselsteiner, one of Austria's most successful entrepreneurs. He was previously an MP for the Liberal Forum, which merged with NEOS in 2014.

First Followers

First followers are trusted acquaintances and colleagues who are ready to help in an unselfish, very hands-on way. Even though everyone does almost everything in a political start-up, not everyone can be chief—you also need people willing to put in lots of hours to do the essential groundwork. They are also very important because they become role models for subsequent followers, and often become campaign staff members or "super volunteers" who manage other volunteers.

To recruit first followers Emmanuel Macron informed his private office at the French Ministry for Finance in Bercy about his plans 1 month ahead of the launch of En Marche. Sandro Martin, who had joined his team 6 months earlier, recalled the moment when I interviewed him at the En Marche headquarter in November 2017. "In March, we had a meeting where he explained the dynamic, and his idea, not to run for office, but to launch a new citizen movement.

I was very enthusiastic about this. For me, it was obvious that for the upcoming presidential elections, we could not have only the candidates who were known to be running at the time. Hollande was running again, you had Sarkozy, Fillon—so it was all the same old politicians who wanted to run again. And since I had seen not only the problems from inside the administration and the private office of the minister, but also the very bad dynamic and political panorama in France, I was very eager to start something new."

A month later, Sandro helped launch "La Grande Marche", the nationwide, door-to-door canvassing that became the first chapter of Macron's success story. Sandro got involved in his neighbourhood in Paris, the 11th arrondisement. During the one-and-a-half months La Grande Marche lasted, he knocked on many, many doors, and he also organised the event in his district. Within just a few weeks, he had evolved from a private aide to the Minister, into a campaign co-ordinator.

5.1.2 Organisational Level

On the organisational level, there are three fields to take into consideration when preparing a political start-up:

- islands of discontent
- strategic partners
- societal stakeholders

Islands of Discontent

Islands of discontent are groups that feel the anger the political entrepreneur wants to tap into. They are, therefore, also islands of potential members, activists and voters. Most likely, they are not formally organised. They may be groups that meet regularly in person, or informal networks connected by mailing lists, Facebook groups and the like. They may be non-political on the surface, and they may even be inactive at the time the political entrepreneur approaches them, but still relatively easily mobilised.

In November, 2011, my wife and I were living in London together with our 6-month-old son. Although my life was full and UK politics was interesting in the early days of the Tories' and Liberal Democrats' coalition government, I still checked Austrian news websites every day. Austrian politics was in a state of hibernation. While the world turned, Austria seemed to stand still. The arteries of political reform were clogged by the umpteenth version of the "Grand Coalition" between Social Democrats and Conservatives. But behind the apparently permanent blockage, anger was mounting. *My* anger was mounting.

I was not alone. From abroad, I joined a Viennese group called "Mir fehlen täglich neu die Worte" ("Words fail me every day anew"), a kind of self-help group of the politically tormented, formed to discuss what could be done. I knew most of the participants from my student council days. The group had a Facebook forum, and met irregularly. I joined their meetings via Skype. I had never been involved in party politics, but this was not the first civic initiative on the political fringes I was involved with. All the others had eventually fizzled out, leaving me more frustrated. "Let's make this one different" I urged my fellow members.

It must have been the third of fourth meeting, when Matthias Strolz made a guest appearance in November, 2011. Strolz and I had met at student council in the 1990s, and had subsequently worked on a few projects together. I liked him, and knew him to be a highly innovative and capable entrepreneur. He was also politically savvy and well-connected. At the meeting, he said that the political landscape in Austria would change radically in the coming years; that the post-war duopoly of Social Democrats and Conservatives was coming to an end; that there were many islands of political discontent like ours, mainly in Vienna, which he was currently linking together. He proposed ideas for a new kind of political movement in Austria that he would lead.

The political entrepreneur's task is to identify these islands of discontent, approach them, as Strolz did, and establish whether they shared a political agenda. The next step is to start building bridges between them, and weave a self-supporting web of relationships on which the future movement can be built.

Strategic Partners

Like any enterprise, political enterprises need strategic partners to succeed. They can be political allies, or professional partners with whom the future start-up will have comprehensive and long-term relationships.

Nowoczesna in Poland entered a strategic partnership with the conservative Civic Platform at the end of 2017. At the time of writing, they have a coalition on the Voivodeship level (the Polish provinces), and the city level. Nowoczesna currently polls around 5%, and Civic Platform around 25%, but, as a coalition, they get a "bonus" of an extra 3–5%, which together brings them in the range of 33–35%. However, such a partnership also poses challenges. Civic Platform are much bigger, so Nowoczesna is at risk of being marginalised. Civic Platform have lots of money, and Nowoczesna very little. "But they need us, and we need them, so we co-operate. I don't know if we will keep it that way in the future, but it could also be a coalition for the EU election in 2019", said Katarzyna Lubnauer, Nowoczesna's Chairwoman, when I spoke to her on Skype in June 2018.

Societal Stakeholders
Finally, there may be formally organised stakeholders in the public, the private and the civic sectors that share interests with the future political start-up. They may be non-governmental organisations, business associations, unions, and the like. Ideally, they are allies, but in any case, they are forces to be reckoned with, so it makes sense to reach out. However, alongside strategic partners, societal stakeholders should be contacted in the later stages of preparation, once the main ideas around policy and organisation have been consolidated. Otherwise, the structural forces of those stakeholders may have too strong an impact on the emerging political start-up.

5.2   Assemble

Joanna Schmidt had been a successful manager in the interior fittings industry and an entrepreneur in the education sector. Now she was the 36-year old Chancellor of the Collegium da Vinci, a private university in Poznań. Like many Poles, the mother of three had been watching the build-up to the Presidential elections in 2015 with some concern. Most of the early polls had predicted that the incumbent, the independent centrist Bronisław Komorowski, would receive the largest vote share in the first round. Some polls even pointed to an outright win, avoiding a second-round run-off.

On 10 May, however, his opponent, Andrzej Duda of the right-wing Law and Justice party, won the first round by a whisker. The second and final round took place 2 weeks later. This time, the polls saw Duda narrowly ahead. On May 24 2015, he gained 51.5% of the vote, making it the closest Presidential election in Polish history. Suddenly, Poland had a right-wing, national-conservative President. The result sent shockwaves throughout Europe. It was only 6 months until the next parliamentary elections, and the governing Civic Platform was in disarray.

That was the day, Joanna Schmidt told me later, she decided to become a political entrepreneur. The thought had been at the back of her mind for nearly 2 years. She did not want a politician like Duda, and the people of Law and Justice, to be responsible for her future and for the future of her children. It was impossible for her to live in Poland and do nothing, criticising but ultimately accepting the changes Duda and others would soon be making.

She was not alone. A couple of days later, her old friend Paweł Rabiej, a Polish journalist and author, called. He and Ryszard Petru, a well-known economist, were looking for an expert in education and higher education policy. They were organising a political gathering in Warsaw, a citizen congress, 1 week after the election, on May 31. The congress was held at the Torwar event centre, opposite the soccer stadium of Legia Warszawa.

That day marked the birth of a new liberal party called Nowoczesna (Polish for "Modern"). They had booked a location with a capacity for 1000 people. A few days before, the number of online registrations obliged them to switch to a much larger venue. In the event, 8000 Poles showed up.

"The Government had not taken the whole thing seriously" Petru would later tell me at the ALDE congress in Amsterdam. "Had they anticipated the sheer size, they could have done something important that day. They didn't. So it was the first news on TV. It was the moment when all of Poland heard about Nowoczesna, and it was the moment of our start."

Assembling is the third step on the road of the political entrepreneur. Getting the band together for the first time is something special. As Hermann Hesse wrote in his philosophical poem "Steps", "Jedem Anfang wohnt ein Zauber inne" ("A magic dwells in each beginning"), and that is certainly true for the first assembly of a political party, even if the turnout is not as huge as in Nowoczesna's case.

However, it is not only magic that dwells in beginnings; there's risk, too. The first assembly means leaving the small circle of conspirators, stepping out of the shadows, and onto the (semi-)public stage. It also means starting to give up a certain amount of control, and trusting the process. Beginnings matter in more ways than one; first assemblies that do not live up to expectations may not be fatal, but because of path dependency, they suggest the movement may not be riding a huge wave after all.

Nowoczesna's first informal assembly, its congress on 31 May 2015 in Warsaw, certainly exceeded expectations. A quote attributed to Woody Allen goes "80% of success is showing up", and by that standard, Nowoczesna set themselves up for a huge success. How did they mobilise 8000 citizens, I asked Malgorzata Bonikowska, the Polish political scientist and publisher who helped organise the event.

"To tell you the truth", she responded thoughtfully when we met at the offices of the parliamentary group of NEOS in Vienna, "it was not hard to mobilise people. People *were mobilised*. People were waiting for something. We are talking about people like us: open-minded, wanting some constructive work to be done, seeing that nothing good is happening, seeing that this present elite is closed down within their own circles. So, people were of course also thinking that PIS is not the party we would like to vote for. So these people just came for the Congress. We has announced that something new was happening, and these people just came! It was not difficult.

It was like—if you just gave them the right product, they were just waiting already for it. You just came at the right moment, because the moment came also with the elections. You know, election time is always the time you can really do something. Because it was just in May, and it was half a year before elections. If it had happened two years before the elections, maybe this potential would have gone nowhere. But just before elections you can play the game; you can propose a new offer, and people can vote. You can test your potential."

At the congress, the first hour was used to allow participants to state their policy suggestions via a microphone, and then pin them to a wall that had "Nowoczesna" written on it. The following hour-and-a-half featured Ryszard Petru speaking and introducing eight other speakers who represented a cross-section of the organisation and elements of Polish society: a doctor, a teacher, a mayor, a youth movement organiser, a businessman and a publicist.

Kairos is an ancient Greek concept that means the right, critical or opportune moment. While Chronos stands for sequential time, Kairos stands for the proper time for action. In the case of Political Entrepreneurship, Kairos is most dependent on elections, as Bonikowska's assessment makes clear. Nowoczesna entered the political arena at a critical moment in time, right after the shock of the election of a right-wing populist President, and only 6 months ahead of the election of a new Parliament. *People were mobilised.* They were waiting for the *right product*. In politics, it has a lot to do with Kairos. You cannot stand back, and wait to ride the next wave. You have to get on it when it's there, and ride it as best you can. It's do or die.

However, if you have the chance, and no elections are just around the corner, you can try to catch the wave earlier. Catching the wave earlier gives you more time to design and build a more resilient organisation. Also, if the wave is not yet so gigantic, falling off doesn't mean sudden death. On the other hand, you cannot be entirely sure the wave you are on will ever grow to a significant size.

That is the gamble NEOS took in 2011, almost 2 years ahead of the next national election. A few days after the meeting where Strolz had presented his initial ideas for a new political movement in Vienna, I called him, and told him I wanted to be part of it. I wanted to contribute whatever I could from London, where I was based at the time, as Director International of the Royal Society of Arts, a charity. He welcomed me on board, and told me there were two others in the co-lead with him: Feri Thierry and Veit Dengler. Feri was a mutual friend of Strolz and myself from the student council, and later became the Executive Director of NEOS. At the time, he was a successful public relations entrepreneur, who took a low-key, but central role in the background, to avoid conflicts of interest with his company.

Veit Dengler had done a lot of research on the founding of new parties. He had even written his thesis on the Social Democrats, a spinoff of the Labour party in the 1980s in the UK. He told me over a coffee at my apartment in Vienna about one of the lessons he learned back then: "If you split off, or found something new, you will attract a lot of crazies. So there needs to be a solid core of people in the leadership team, and there needs to be a solid programmatic core. If you found first and write your programme later, the risk that it gets hijacked by crazies is too high. So we started by assembling this first group."

Strolz, Dengler and Thierry met three or four times, to discuss how they wanted to proceed. One of the meetings was with Erhard Busek, a former ÖVP Chairman and Vice-Chancellor of Austria, and long-time mentor of Strolz. "Erhard", Dengler remembered, "said something like, 'nice idea, but you have *neither* money *nor* celebrities. You need either money or celebrities, otherwise it won't work.'" They decided to give it a go, nonetheless.

The MIT-based action researcher Otto Scharmer calls this critical stage of assembling this first small group "crystallising". Their purpose and dedication decide much of the fate of the political enterprise: "When a small group of key persons commits itself to the purpose and outcomes of a project, the power of their intention creates an energy field that attracts people, opportunities, and resources that make things happen. This core group functions as a vehicle for the whole to manifest" (op. cit.).

This first assembly, Strolz told me on the phone at the end of 2011, would take place in February, 2012, overnight at a conference hotel outside of Vienna. It was a first test: could they mobilise enough interesting people? The idea was to have 15–20 participants (compare that to Nowoczesna's 8000!), friends and friends of friends. I would be one of the facilitators, a role I was well-acquainted with from my work as seminar trainer and coach earlier in my life. We started planning and designing.

About a month before the gathering, Strolz said that there was more interest in the project than he had previously thought, and that we had to change our design to accommodate 40 people. I remember challenging him on this. I argued 20 people were more than enough—better to have a small core group of trusted friends, than to have 40 of whom some would probably soon drop out, or leak confidential information. Strolz disagreed: "Go with the flow", he said. "If the dynamics bring us 40 people, that's good, so let's work with 40."

Today, I know he was right. I wanted to keep the circle small, because I wanted to be one of the chosen few, not because I really thought 20 was better than 40. In fact, most of the 40 are still with NEOS today. My ego got in the way. Accommodating a larger group is just a question of method. Also, it meant that because that group would form the core group of NEOS, we started to work with large-group methods right from the beginning. That was formative for the movement as a whole. As I said earlier, beginnings matter, particularly when political entrepreneurs assemble.

What are the critical elements in getting the beginning in such a large group-setting right? A certain homogeneity of the group, in terms of personal values, age and sociodemographic background (diversity becomes mission-critical later); mutual trust, fun, and a tight workshop design, with a clear focus.

Still, there was plenty of diversity. We made the decision to confront that right at the beginning, when we opened with a systemic constellation exercise where we asked people to position themselves in the room according to questions like "Who did you vote for in the past?" or "Are you in favour or opposed to an inheritance tax?" There were people present who were more conservative-leaning, green, or with a liberal political background. There were others with no political background whatsoever, people who were in favour of inheritance tax, and people who were against it. The exercise was fun, and became a kind of template for the gatherings that followed.

"We came out of the retreat with a relatively high level of euphoria" Dengler recalled. "Among the 40 participants, there were a lot of intellectually and professionally exciting people, and lots of entrepreneurial energy."

To him, "the first criterion of success of a start-up is that you need people with an incredible amount of energy, but also a certain naivety that makes them want to run through the wall. If you don't have that, you cannot be successful as a start-up." He said this outlook was often found in people who have entrepreneurial backgrounds.

One of those entrepreneurs was Michael Schiebel, who would later become Political Director and Parliamentary Group Director of NEOS. The tall and calm Salzburgian had already been Group Director of the Liberal Forum in the 1990s, which would later run on an electoral platform with NEOS and merge with it in 2014. He was the one who closed down the shop when the Liberal Forum failed to return to Parliament in 1999. He had met Dengler through his wife, Karin Doppelbauer, who worked with Dengler at Dell in Bratislava, and who would later become a Founding Board Member of NEOS and, subsequently, one of their MPs. At the assembly, Schiebel was one of the most politically experienced. "I think I was one of the oldest at the gathering", Schiebel said when I talked with him in Vienna in February 2018, "and perhaps a little more disillusioned than others there. On the first day, my job was to infuse a dose of scepticism, particularly about political platforms that remain in the realm of civil society: 'not another one of those' I thought. And founding a new party? Lots of challenges, very difficult to build it from scratch and to empower it.

At the end of the first day, half of my scepticism had eroded. Why? Lots of different people invest one and a half days of their time, to discuss with each other, and while they had differing opinions, it was the tone that did it for me. That was later called appreciation. I thought that that had a genuinely new quality if people really talk to each other and tackle problems together. So I thought, just looking at the substance, there might be chance."

But there were still plenty of challenges ahead, like "organisational questions, the second big hurdle. When nobody has time, such projects tend to fade away. It was a time when a few new start-ups were in the pipeline—like the Pirates and Team Stronach. But much to my surprise", Schiebel recalled, "I was captivated by the idea on the second day. As I was self-employed, I could see myself freeing up time to engage. At the end of the meeting, I volunteered to lead the five policy task forces—Europe, Education, Democracy, Economy and Social systems. A couple of months later Environment was added as well."

The other project he took over, because of his prior experience in politics, was the task force on statutes.

"So following the first gathering of the group in the Helenental in Lower Austria, I was getting deeply involved. I had not expected that, when I arrived for the weekend. But it was great. Good times, good weekend. In a way I had the experience of an alcoholic who had been sober for 12 years, and who had been slipped a pack of rum balls", he laughed.

Strolz and Dengler decided there was a large enough core group of people who were ready to drive the project, and who had the energy and start-up mentality that could actually make it work.

As Beate Meinl-Reisinger, who would later become Chairwoman of NEOS Vienna before becoming Chairwoman and Group Leader of NEOS, recalled, when I spoke to her in Vienna in January 2018: "I was there, and I was taken with the people there. It felt good. I knew many of them. I was delighted to see people who I had not known were involved with the project. It was a little bit like a class reunion. People around the same age, academic background, pro-European attitude, résumés that had been in touch with politics, some closer, some further, lots of Alpbach [a yearly political conference in the Austrian Alps]. It was a very enjoyable group."

But Beate also had some afterthoughts that exemplified the agonies and temptations political entrepreneurs often endure. "I also said, however, that I was pregnant, that I had to give birth, see if the child is healthy, and only then could make a decision. Family comes first. And that is how it happened."

She was still employed by the ÖVP at the time, but on maternity leave. "I remember an interview [at ÖVP] about my professional future after the maternity leave. Since they had no plans and ideas at all for my future development it wasn't hard for me to say goodbye."

She didn't become deeply involved until summer, 2012, after she had a conversation with Strolz about how she could contribute.

"With two little children, you have to ask yourself whether you want to take such a risk—to co-found something really new, and with it stick the finger up to your whole professional network. At that point I had a call from the ÖVP about an opening as a Head of Department in a Ministry that would fit my profile very well. I remember I was at my parents', and my father urged me to accept. He said it a great opportunity—international, and a secure job with my two little kids. I paused and reflected.

But the rebellion won. After all, I wanted to get a job because of my skills and abilities, not because of party affiliation. So I started my rebellion against the way Austrian politics operated.

Around that time I was at the European Forum Alpbach, and I bumped into a politician of the ÖVP. He asked me, what I was up to these days? I said, I would join Matthias Strolz and his movement. He yelled at me, 'you folks, you first have to try to reform parties from within!' And I thought, 'that's the very reason I am doing this.' We had all tried reforming from within."

Yesh Atid, the Israeli centrist start-up, chose another approach for assembling. Yair Lapid, its charismatic founder, did not want to take the risk of organising a first gathering, and nobody or too few people showing up. After all, he was a well-known former TV presenter and anchor of the leading news show in Israel. The advantage of being in the public eye would be an immediate weakness if the kick-off proved a damp squib. The press would mock him. After all, there had been speculation in the media about him founding a new party for 2 years before he announced it.

Lapid decided to organise the first assembly without attracting media attention, to test the water, and see if there was enough civic interest. The first meeting was held outside Tel Aviv, away from the media. They invited 20 people; 75 came, and talked until 2 am. Lapid concluded there was enough interest to take the political enterprise public. The next meeting was also held outside Tel Aviv, but they invited the media. All of a sudden, 500 people showed up. Now they knew they had something special on their hands. A year later, Yesh Atid entered the Knesset as the second largest party with a 14.3% share of the vote.

Emmanuel Macron took perhaps the most well-prepared approach of all. On April 6, 2016, he hosted a "citizen's rally" in his hometown of Amiens, in Northern France. In front of the press, he announced that he was founding a new political movement called "En Marche". As serving Economy Minister of France, he immediately made headlines in the national and international press. He presented En Marche as open to anyone from any political party, and as already rounding up funding and support among MPs. Its aim, he said, was to come up with new ideas to solve the "blockages" holding France back. Ten days later, on Saturday April 16, 2016, the training of field organisers started.

The initial assembling does not have to be on the ground, to be effective. Social networks like Facebook allow for the creation of open or closed virtual groups whose members may have never met in person. Recently, there have been attempts to assemble political start-ups via Twitter. The early Pirate Parties, the first one founded in Sweden in 2006, were political entrepreneurs ahead of their time with their digital approach to politics, and technology-supported processes like "Liquid Democracy". It will be interesting to see which fully virtual political start-up will be the first to succeed. Volt, a pan-European, progressive movement aiming to revolutionise the way politics is done across Europe, is one of the contenders. But local "off-line" politics seems unlikely to become redundant anytime soon.

(Co)-Design

6

> *You never change things by fighting the existing reality. To change something, build a new model that makes the existing model obsolete.*
>
> Attributed to Buckminster Fuller

Political enterprises can be initiated top-down or bottom-up. En Marche, for example, was launched top-down by a popular finance minister while still in office. Ciudadanos was launched by 15 well-known Catalan intellectuals, journalists and lawyers via a manifesto in the media. Ryszard Petru of Nowoczesna was a highly reputed economist who frequently appeared in the media. NEOS, on the other hand, was launched by 40 citizens nobody knew. Similarly, Momentum, was launched by a group of young activists unknown to the public.

Having a public platform and a media megaphone helps to get a quick start, but it puts you under immediate scrutiny. Less scrutiny gives you more freedom on policy and organisation design. You have to be more inclusive, and it may take you longer, but co-designing the political enterprise may ultimately lead a more resilient organisation.

There is no right or wrong way.

The Austrian economist and social reformer, Otto Neurath, once said of the *conditio humana*:

> There is no blank slate. We are like skippers who have to re-build their ship on the open sea, without ever being able to disassemble it in the docks, and build it anew with the best parts. ("Otto Neurath: Eine politische Biografie", Günther Sandner, Zsolnay, 2014).

This is obviously true for traditional political parties. You cannot simply take them "to the dock". You have to re-build them at sea. But it does not apply so much to new parties. Even if path dependency means you do not start with a blank slate, you have many more degrees of freedom, and there are dry docks. The docks are where you design your ship, and build it with the best parts you can get. The docks

© Springer Nature Switzerland AG 2019
J. Lentsch, *Political Entrepreneurship*,
https://doi.org/10.1007/978-3-030-02861-9_6

are from where you embark on your maiden voyage, sailing into the vast ocean of politics.

Another difference between traditional political parties and start-ups is the latter's bewildering array of choices. Starting from scratch means you do not need to account for legacy structures, vested interests or skeletons in the closet. I believe this is one of the major contributions of political entrepreneurs to a system's transformation: they challenge all kinds of orthodoxies about how a political party should be organised. The truth is many traditional parties would have failed long ago, were it not for the historically high barriers to entry into the political market. But technology and other factors have dramatically reduced such barriers. If the barriers to entry crumble, you need to adapt. That need for adaptation applies to your strategy as much as to your structure, culture and policies. It applies to the whole political organisation.

As Naomi Stanford wrote in her book "Guide to Organisation Design: Creating high performing and adaptable enterprises" (Profile Books, 2007):

> Organisation design means holistic thinking about the organisation: its systems, structures, people, performance measures, processes and culture, and the way the whole operates in the environment.

> Organisation design happens as much through social interactions and conversations as through planning.

> Organisation design is a fundamental, continuing process, not a repair job.

Organisation design remains one of the least developed disciplines in politics.

Coming back to the aforementioned Buckminster Fuller quote, organisation design allows political entrepreneurs to show how the existing model of politics on a large scale can be made obsolete, by demonstrating, on a small scale, a new design, better adapted to the modern environment.

Over the next several pages, I will present the choices facing political entrepreneurs as they set about designing their political enterprise. I will give practical examples of how the start-ups depicted in this book have dealt with them, and what differentiates them from traditional parties.

6.1   Continuous Learning and Transformation

According to Peter Senge, pioneer of the systems view of organisations: "The only sustainable competitive advantage is an organisation's ability to learn faster than the competition" (The Fifth Discipline: The Art and Practice of the Learning Organization, Doubleday/Currency, 1990).

Societies are changing at a faster pace than ever before. Humans today have access to much more powerful technology than they did just a couple of decades ago. The same goes for enterprises. The median age of the world's most valuable companies was 20 in 2016. What works today might be yesterday's news tomorrow.

Start-ups therefore need to innovate relentlessly. To transform the markets around them, they need to keep transforming themselves. To evolve, they need to learn continuously. As AirBnB Founder Brian Chesky said: to keep growing, "you can't stay the same" ("Airbnb's ambitious second act will take it way beyond couch surfing", Katrina Brooker, Vanity Fair, November, 2016).

Politics might be slower to adapt than businesses, and political parties have more inertia for good reasons. But why should politics be totally inert? A political enterprise can only be successful if it cultivates what Peter Senge called "The Art and Practice of the Learning Organisation".

I interviewed the Polish political scientist and publisher Małgorzata Bonikowska in Vienna in February 2017. She told me the main reason behind the downfall of the centrist Civic Platform in 2015 was that it *stopped learning*. "It didn't happen immediately, but while in power, both parties in Coalition, Civic Platform and the People's Party PSL, became their own bubble. It was like a closed circle. And within the parties themselves, especially Civic Platform, there were not many newcomers with new ideas. They had good advisers, who made very good analyses, but nothing more than that. It was just paper.

And even the electorate, the business leaders, top people in business, they were all suggesting something. This was a party of small and medium and big business as well. These people were voting for this party. And there was no response. Even within the party, there were pleas to be more open, to have dialogue with people, to go out of Warsaw. But there was less and less interest. Why? Because once you are in power, you lose orientation. You are so used to being a minister or a parliamentarian that ordinary people don't interest you anymore."

She told me there were many circles in Poland, in the small towns, in the villages, in small businesses, where people felt neglected. "People were feeling that nothing was good for them—maybe things were good for the elites, but not for them. And at the same time, the [right-wing, national-conservative] PIS was such an opposition that Civic Platform thought Poles would never vote for it. So this was their argument: you may not like us, but who else? And this is why they were blind to the reality." With their heads buried in the sand, they didn't see what was coming.

That ignorance and lack of alertness gave PIS the upper hand, leading to the victories of Andrzej Duda in the presidential election, and of the party in the parliamentary elections in 2015. A shape of things that at the time were yet to come in Europe with Brexit, and in the US with the election of Donald Trump. But at the same time, Civic Platform's failure opened up a window of opportunity in the political centre for the political start-up, Nowoczesna.

My point here is that Civic Platform failed, because it didn't realise that continuous technology-assisted learning is a core discipline for twenty-first century political enterprises.

In France, En Marche has taken technology-assisted continuous learning to a new level—internally, by deploying formats such as Massively Open Online Courses (MOOCs—see page 53), and externally, through dialogue with citizens. Following their "La Grande Marche" exercise, they are currently training activists as pollsters, to turn France into one gigantic focus group. In a speech in 1882, "Qu'est-ce qu'une nation?" ("What is a Nation?"), the French philosopher and historian Ernest Renan defined a nation as "un plébiscite de tous les jours" (a daily plebiscite). It seems the vision of En Marche is knowing how citizens *would* vote on various issues in this metaphorical plebiscite in real-time. But the idea is not to use the information gained to tell the people what they want to hear. It's to lead with more empathy.

To be a sustainable political enterprise, it's no longer enough to learn and adapt from time to time. You have to be learning and adapting constantly.

Traditional parties have a cycle of updating their programmes that can be measured in decades. One update cycle may easily take a year or two. That also applies to their structures. This frequency is reminiscent of Microsoft Windows in the 1990s, when it took 3 years from Windows 95 to Windows 98. This is not how you do things anymore in the age of Open Source.

At NEOS, for example, everything is in "permanent beta"—never completed, always open to adaptation. There is constant rapid updating. And it is not just the selected few systems architects who are working to improve the platform as a whole, while the others are just tinkering around the edges. Position papers are being written collaboratively, in network-based task forces, by staff, volunteers and experts. The drafts are then peer-reviewed on an open source platform called "motion forge", in a standardised process with feedback loops built in.

To keep up these rapid manifesto update cycles NEOS convenes two or more member assemblies per year, where the final versions of position papers are debated. That points to another difference: at most party conferences delegates represent the party membership. At NEOS member assemblies, party members represent themselves.

6.2   Fundraising

A political start-up needs money. "What we learned from the first election campaign was that it is incredibly important to have enough fundraising capacity. You need one person to drive the others, and a large enough network" said Michael Bernhard, NEOS's financial office, when I talked to him in the offices of the NEOS parliamentary group in June 2018. "But fundraising also has to be a top-priority for the leaders, whether or not there are elections. You can hire someone for the operational stuff, but this person won't bring in millions. So, at election time, the responsibility for fund-raising must also lie with the frontrunner, and it must lie with the Chairperson all the time."

Bernhard emphasised that, to be an effective fundraiser, the frontrunner needs to believe the party will succeed. "People sense if you have someone who does not really want to win. Money is another expression of time. If they do not feel the frontrunner's seriousness and inner belief, or they see a careerist sitting in front of them who may win but lacks conviction, they will ask themselves why should they support the campaign."

But perhaps the greatest contribution party leaders can make to fundraising campaigns is to help develop an attractive set of policies. As a marketer whose name escapes me said many years ago: "scratch a good marketing campaign, and you'll find a good product."

6.2.1 Incentivise Party Members

Bernhard's advice for political entrepreneurs is to "build strongly on your own base. If your own movement constituents believe in their success, they will also make financial contributions big and small. And if your own people fund you, others will follow."

To incentivise party members, NEOS introduced a highly successful instrument right at the beginning: risk-carrying private loans from supporters. In essence, these were donations that converted into loans that would be paid back if and when NEOS entered Parliament at a national or state level from the public funding it will then receive. Bernhard said these convertible donations work very well as long as people believe you have a fair chance of getting in. "For the last parliamentary election in 2017, we are looking at a total sum of €600,000 from that alone. There were members who loaned us up to €250,000" he said. The success of this innovation means that NEOS won't need banks to finance the next parliamentary election campaign. "People must believe you will be successful" Bernhard emphasises, "but that's no different from banks, of course. In fact, their risk management systems assess risk even more conservatively than party members."

As in business, so in politics, credibility is the key to successful risk assessment.

6.2.2 High-Net-Worth Individuals

Having a billionaire among your supporters helps. But the trust required for a large donation won't be won with a single pitch or with the presentation of a political vision. "That trust you earn through hard work, over years", said Bernhard. "You must not forget, people like that have to deal with supplicants who are after their money every single day. That means they are always checking whether the cause is for real, or not."

In the case of NEOS, Hans-Peter Haselsteiner, one of Austria's most successful and well-known entrepreneurs, had been a Liberal Forum member of parliament in the 1990s. But it had taken Angelika Mlinar, then Chairwoman of the Liberal Forum and later President of NEOS Lab and Vice-Chairwoman of NEOS, years to establish a trusting relationship with him.

When the Liberal Forum was in severe financial trouble in 2010, Haselsteiner offered support on the condition that Bernhard managed to resolve more than 50% of its liabilities. He would then pay for the other half. "I took on that task, which cost me several months of my life" said Bernhard. When he finally managed to achieve the target a fruitful professional relationship began. But credibility has to be earned anew for every election when support is asked for.

6.2.3   Relations with Pollsters

One key factor in gaining that credibility are polls. An intimate and constant exchange with the pollsters is, therefore, crucial.

"In a small a country, such as Austria, there are no more than five or six pollsters who are questioned by potential donors" said Bernhard. "Not surprisingly, the donors want to validate what we tell them. If the pollster they trust tells them that we will not be successful in the election, the donation is dead. That means public opinion, and pollsters who measure it, have to be constantly cultivated."

6.2.4   Incentivise Regional Organisations

All parts of the organisation must be motivated to throw their weight behind fundraising. The trick here is to make the support of the national party dependent on the fundraising success of the state or regional organisations. This rule must then be applied to all organisations in the same way.

"The logic henceforth was that for every Euro raised by the state group, the national party would contribute 50 cents in the form of a loan" Bernhard explained. "So two thirds have to be raised by the state group, one third comes from the national party."

6.3   Openness and Transparency

Many of our current political systems suffer from a lack of transparency. On the individual level, this leads to a lack of accountability, and on the systemic level, to too many career politicians, corruption, and consequently angry and distrustful citizens. Political start-ups can differentiate themselves by aiming for more openness and transparency. The two terms are closely linked, but there are different concepts that political start-ups can use when designing their organisations.

6.3.1   Openness

Openness is the default of the twenty-first century world. The "Open Source Initiative" before the turn of the millennium championed Open Source software developed *by* and *for* the user community; it had a huge impact. Its principles were not only modelled on global collaborative ventures, such as Linux, Creative Commons and Wikipedia, but became guiding lights for twenty-first century politics. As stated on the OpenSource.com website, (https://opensource.com/open-source-way), they include:

Open Exchange
We can learn more from each other when information is open. A free exchange of ideas is critical to creating an environment where people are allowed to learn and use existing information toward creating new ideas.

Participation
When we are free to collaborate, we create. We can solve problems that no one person may be able to solve on their own.

Rapid Prototyping
Rapid prototypes can lead to rapid failures, but that leads to better solutions found faster. When you're free to experiment, you can look at problems in new ways and look for answers in new places. You can learn by doing.

Meritocracy
In a meritocracy, the best ideas win. In a meritocracy, everyone has access to the same information. Successful work determines which projects rise and gather effort from the community.

Community
Communities are formed around a common purpose. They bring together diverse ideas and share work. Together, a global community can create beyond the capabilities of any one individual. It multiplies effort and shares the work. Together, we can do more.

How can these principles be embedded in an organisational design?

NEOS operates a nationwide online forum (currently in the form of a Facebook group) with more than 1000 members and activists. There is open exchange within the community every day. Everyone is in there and can be reached, including the Chairwoman.

NEOS also runs open primaries. Any citizen can participate, as a voter and as a candidate. It is a three-step open process. The public is invited to vote on the list of candidates, and thousands do. Then, the board of NEOS votes. As a third and last step, all members have a vote. The results are tallied and the overall ranking of candidates determined by the total of all three rounds. NEOS only conducts these primaries at the national, European, regional and municipal levels.

Most events are public and live-streamed, to allow for open exchange independent of location.

To enable rapid prototyping, En Marche first collected citizens' ideas on a nationwide level in La Grande Marche. Based on the insights gained, Macron made thematic speeches, which were in turn commented on by 4000 local committees. In the light of these comments, programme papers were incrementally improved. Every member can form a local En Marche committee. He or she is free to run events, invite others to join, and build a community.

There are many other examples of political start-ups embedding openness in their organisational design. There are also differences; some are more open, some less so. But together, they add up to an underlying philosophy that could be called "open source politics".

Openness alone does not guarantee electoral success for political start-ups, as the now mostly defunct Pirate Parties of the early twenty-first century can attest. Starting with the first Pirate Party in Sweden in 2006, they tried to design political parties in a radically open way, with few or no hierarchies at all. Consequently, they encountered problems in making decisions efficiently. The political start-ups portrayed in this book are, to use a metaphor from Eric S. Raymond's book *The Cathedral and the Bazaar: Musings on Linux and Open Source by an Accidental Revolutionary* (O'Reilly Media, 1999), "Cathedrals" and "Bazaars" at the same time. They are open, yet they have hierarchies. They are about leadership *and* participation. Sometimes these two clash. But openness is a powerful principle that harnesses collective intelligence as much as it serves as a differentiator for traditional parties. Most importantly, it fosters civic engagement by lowering the barriers to entry into the political world. It opens up a new supply chain of ideas. After all, "All of us are smarter than one of us" (anon).

6.3.2 Transparency

Louis Brandeis, the distinguished American lawyer and Associate Justice on the US Supreme Court, wrote in 1914 that: "Sunlight is the best disinfectant." That's as true today as it was then, and no less so in politics.

"We decided to finance our activities with 'clean money', transparently", Ivan Stefunko, Co-Founder of Progressive Slovakia, told me during our Skype interview in April, 2018. "In Slovakia, every party has some oligarchs behind it, with very clear interests in receiving some kind of state aid or subsidy. So we put together five people including myself willing to invest at least €200,000 each in the start-up phase. For Slovakia, that's a lot. The other four were entrepreneurs as well, like Michal Truban, the founder of a web hosting service, and Michal Meško, the founder of the biggest Slovak bookstore. Of course, in the meantime we have started to raise funds transparently from other people as well." In a country like Slovakia where corruption is still widespread that already amounted to a small revolution.

Beate Meinl-Reisinger, at the time of writing Chairwoman of NEOS Vienna and now Chairwoman of NEOS, told me of her experience with the party she worked with previously, the ÖVP. "As a party, at some point you have to read the signs of the times. You cannot *not* disclose who is funding you, and through what channels. But when I asked, I was met with polite incomprehension."

Most of our political systems and our traditional political parties are designed to be opaque. Even party members often cannot get the full picture, let alone citizens. The consequences are unaccountable political leaders, and parties where backroom deals are the norm. More transparency leads to increased accountability. When you need to declare your interests, you cannot hide things in plain sight.

Transparency is a competitive advantage, but comes with a price, as NEOS financial officer, Michael Bernhard explained.

"When I came into politics, around 2010 with the Liberal Forum [later merged with NEOS], it was known that Governors at state-level were handed envelopes with money at meetings. Politics was for sale, even then. Our decision to be fully transparent led to the situation where we got significantly *less* money than others. But we were always on the safe side. We never had to be afraid someone would dish the dirt on us and thus destroy us shortly after our first success. You only get this kind of 'not for sale' reputation if you are fully transparent. For financial officers this is not always fun, because we tend to like money. But it is vital for the survival of a young movement."

The political reality is that legal requirements are often still very lax. In Austria, NEOS provides transparency well beyond what is legally required. To date it is the only parliamentary party to offer real-time transparency (in practice, with a time lag of a few weeks, for accounting reasons). All revenues including donations, but also all expenses, from travel to office supplies, are listed on a public website. That applies as much to the party as it does to the parliamentary group and the Lab. This information is provided as Open data on the public platform Open Data Portal Austria (http://data.opendataportal.at/dataset?q=neos&sort=score+desc%2C+name+asc).   No   other Austrian parliamentary party so far has been willing to follow suit.

6.4   Unity in Diversity

Traditional parties were designed in the nineteenth or twentieth century, and for the most part have grown organically since then. Radical organisational re-designs are rare. Some argue that it is a testament to the resilience of parties. I argue that it's a sign of the protection they enjoy, by virtue of the very high barriers to entry for new parties.

Every organisation is a creature of its context. Those political parties were designed to be adapted to the societies of their time, which look rather different from today's societies. Although there have been many changes and organisational reforms, the interests vested in the formalised sub-sections, internal unions, federal branches and other organisational features within parties, often produce a cacophony rather than a finely orchestrated piece. This makes leadership almost impossible, because instead of the best people, those with the right geographical or sub-organisational affiliations are promoted. Thus, the party apparatus itself has become part of the problem that prevents democracies from meeting voters' expectations.

The alternative model *du jour* is authoritarian: instead of the leadership of no one where organisational arithmetic trumps everything else, it offers the leadership of one, where the leader's opinion determines outcomes.

Both models, for obvious reasons, are problematic. Developing a third model would mean having leadership as well as participation, and safeguarding both unity and diversity, instead of playing them off against each other.

I would call this form of organisational model a "Breathing Organisation". It would allow the organisation to get together in unity in decision-making (breathing in), while at the same time allowing for a diversity of perspectives that feed into the process of getting there. It would allow for a high degree of individual freedom and autonomy (breathing out).

This has structural and cultural implications. For one, it needs to be a partially hierarchical, and a partially networked structure; a *hybrid* structure. Hierarchy alone does not provide enough freedom or flexibility. A network alone does not allow for enough unity, as the Pirate Parties have demonstrated ("Are Pirate Parties relevant to European politics?", Iva Kopraleva, European Council on Foreign Relations, January 20, 2017).

NEOS, for example, tries to resolve this "as well as" challenge by being structured as only one legal entity. Branch parties on the regional and communal level are not legal entities in their own right. In that sense, NEOS is highly centralised. On the other hand, the highest strategic body of the organisation is the Extended Board with 28 members—rather large for a small party—which gives regional representatives quite a lot of power. Members also have more power than in other parties, because the member assemblies consist of individual representatives, rather than delegates.

This "One NEOS"-policy, extends beyond the structure, into the collaborative culture of the organisation. Elections, for example, wherever they may be, are *everyone's priority*. While compliance rules are always observed, people at NEOS help each other out. This also applies to the executive level. For example, in 2014, an informal group called the "co-ordination round" was established, without formal power, for the Directors of the party, the parliamentary group and the academy to align themselves on a bi-weekly basis. Since then, it has become a backbone not only for handling operational management, but for the organisation as a whole.

6.5   Controlling

The "unity in diversity" design described above has an important catch: since it is the only legal entity, the national party is ultimately liable for financial decisions made at all levels of the organisation.

"You need very strict rules" Michael Bernhard told me, particularly in election campaigns when emotions are running high. "Top candidates will always say they need more money. You also need a counter-signer for approving invoices above a certain threshold; we set that at €10,000. People are very passionate during a campaign. That must not lead to a weakened movement after the election, because of overspending."

At the beginning, NEOS had no formal rules. Lots of things got authorised that were only discovered weeks or months later. After the national elections in 2013, that led to massive internal conflicts. In fact, it almost killed the political start-up. "It probably took NEOS 3 years to recover fully financially, and regain its full strength" said Bernhard. "The all-time peak of debts, following the European elections in

2014, was almost €4 million. That's 3 full years of public party funding. But in the meantime we had to start preparing for the next election, which meant we couldn't afford a lot of personnel."

The resulting austerity package was brutal, and left the national party incapable of providing core support services for the build-up of the organisation on a regional level. Work morale among the remaining staff was low because of the pressures, and some left. With better control from the beginning, that might have been avoided.

It took NEOS some time to introduce rigorous financial controls. Bernhard said the turning point was the Carinthian communal elections in 2015.

"We only got six seats, but amassed debts of more than €200,000. We had guidelines for approving expenditure by the Speaker of the state group. But he later claimed that the approvals sent from his laptop were not his, and must have been given by someone else. He further claimed that his laptop was not password-protected, so really anyone in the office could have done it. We realised we needed strict rules to prevent cop-outs.

So we put together financial regulations for all levels of the party: who needs to sign, who needs to approve, the 'four eyes-principle', and so on. That led to a significant reduction of money lost. For regional-level campaigns, there now needs to be a budget that has to be approved by the members' assembly of that region. So members know what to expect, and the state group is accountable to them, and to the national party."

They still find mistakes, Bernhard told me, but they find them during the campaign, not afterwards, so they can be addressed right away.

In 2018, new Managing Directors at state level were introduced, who are directly employed by the national party. That is also supposed to improve control.

Has he, in his role, ever regretted the "One NEOS" policy, I ask Bernhard. It seemed to me that taking ultimate responsibility for the decisions made elsewhere might be hard to swallow at times.

"In realpolitik, you cannot let a state group go bust" he replied. "Take Styria. They ran, but didn't make it, and had €200,000 of debt. If we hadn't supported them, the press would write 'NEOS Styria is bankrupt'. You cannot have that. That would cause such damage to the brand that the whole organisation would have to shut down. It's not an option. For lawyers maybe, but not in reality. The national party has such a huge interest in avoiding such a situation that it will inject money.

If that option didn't exist, however, the question to ask is what a separate legal entity would actually achieve? Separate legal entities would mean groups that were dissatisfied could split off, while keeping the brand, the money, and so on. The fate of the Liberal Forum in the late 90s and early 2000s is instructive: a bankrupt national party on one side, and on the other, a fully financed Viennese state party that refused to help the national party, and dug its own grave in so doing. That could happen again."

Bernhard came to NEOS from the Liberal Forum. It had been in Parliament from 1994–1999, but had only been represented at state level since then. The state parties were separate legal entities, and as Bernhard recalled, that caused an ultimately fatal conflict with the national party.

"What we, as the Liberal Forum, brought to the table" said Bernhard, recalling the NEOS and Liberal Forum merger, "in addition to some generous funders and activists, was 20 years of experience in how *not* to do it. Which is why we advocated for one legal entity early on. All the others who did not do it like that had the same problems: the Pirates, the BZÖ, the Team Stronach, they all wrestled with that. In a party, there are two main reasons for conflict: money and mandates. With the 'One NEOS' policy, we partially circumvented that."

6.6   Exponential Growth

One reason for En Marche's astonishing success in France's Presidential and National Assembly elections in 2017, is that before the elections the party built the most sophisticated digital infrastructure in French political history. Julien Tassy, at the time of writing Director of Marketing and Digital at En Marche, told me how they did it.

"We started with the simple idea that we had to set up something that was very easy for people to use, and very horizontal in the decision making."

Julien worked at Warner Bros. before, as Senior Digital Platform Manager. He joined En Marche to help set up what they called the "Comités Locaux" (local committees). "Every member could set up such a committee, and was free to organise local events and recruit regulars. The idea was to build a digital infrastructure that helped members create those local structures themselves, rather than leaving it to the headquarters to say "we need a structure there, there, and there".

But headquarters helped. They built a map tool where, after a simple validation process, members could easily set up their local committee, or see whether there was one nearby they could join. A principle here was that it should be just as easy to leave the platform, as to join it. "Freedom to be in, freedom to be out" said Tassy. "We needed a platform to be as flexible as possible, because the easier it is for people to leave, the easier it is for people to join".

On top of that tool, Tassy and his team built a Customer Relationship Management system (CRM), to allow members to contact other members, and inform them about their activities. Normally, you have CRM first, and tools second. En Marche turned that orthodoxy on its head. After all, that was one of the reasons a lot of those digital platforms did not work well: you had to adjust to the logic of the system, instead of a system that really fit the logic of the user. "It was a little buggy, at times very buggy, but it was a very simple CRM system for people who created the cells. We didn't create a CRM for ourselves, so we could shoot emails to people. We created a CRM for members, so they could contact other members nearby."

For data protection reasons, however, the system did not give personal information away. "Members couldn't have access to personal information on people they really didn't know, but they could send them invitations to join them, go to a meeting and stuff like that" Tassy explained.

They sent marketing material to their members, saying "there is a committee near you, and here is the link to the map. If there is no committee near you, here is how to create one." They did that for about 2 months. At the end, En Marche had 4000 local committees across France, with tens of thousands of members. Within a few months, En Marche had grown exponentially. It had developed local structures through empowered, self-organisation.

Like En Marche, designing political start-ups for exponential growth means designing them, at least partially, as a network of real-life, digitally supported, highly self-organising networks. But a structure growing this fast needs to be maintained, or it will implode, with potential collateral damage.

So, the local committees were engaged with organising gatherings around Macron's speeches, providing feedback on them, and helping with campaign work. The huge numbers of local activists also created huge training and development opportunities, ideally everywhere and all at the same time. To roll training out across the country, they made some of the training accessible, at any time, in any place. They started to experiment with e-learning formats, and rolled out micro-learning courses as well as a Massive Open Online Course (MOOC).

At the time of writing they were also setting up a platform on which members can set up recurring activities in their communities, say, cleaning the playground on a weekly basis, and inviting other members to join them. This is another example of lateral mobilisation.

To make these platforms easily accessible, Tassy and his team created a single sign-on for En Marche members. "The main idea is to have that freedom of creation, but try to figure out a way for that to be organised, to be documented, and to focus on building the tools which are going to help maintain, open and build this new way of doing politics."

6.7   Brand Differentiation

Building a well-known brand is essential for the success of a political start-up. It takes time and lots of human resources, and it costs *a lot*. The brands of traditional parties are known by close to 100% of the voter population—but for the most part, they're boring. For political start-ups, this is a great opportunity.

"It was very difficult to find a proper name", the Hungarian Andras Fekete-Györ, Chairman of Momentum, told me during our interview at the ALDE congress in Amsterdam in 2017. They wanted to differentiate their movement from FIDESZ, the right-wing nationalist party of Viktor Orbán, and from other existing Hungarian parties. They wanted something clearly internationalist and cosmopolitan, and dithered between "Millennium", most of them being members of the similarly called generation, and "Momentum". They liked the dynamic in the idea of momentum. It was an historic moment they wanted to seize. So they decided to go with it.

Michael Schuster is a successful entrepreneur and venture capitalist in Austria. He was part of the core group of the 40 people who helped prepare what would become NEOS. He also had an indirect role in naming it. He was on vacation with his partner in Spain. They went for a walk, and started brainstorming. It should be different, and not another "The XY Party", or another party named after a colour. It should be new, and should relate to Austria. Suddenly his then partner stopped, and said "NEOS!" *Neos* is Greek for "new", but OS is also the International Air Transport Association abbreviation for Austria. So NEOS could also be read as "New Austria". That's how the communication group, led by Feri Thierry, got to the full name of "NEOS—The New Austria".

That NEOS in combination with liberal, equals "neoliberal", these days a political battle cry of the Left almost devoid of meaning, but nonetheless toxic, gave us some headaches later, but we never looked back.

Colours also signify political movements. That, funnily enough, was a tougher nut to crack. One debate was around breaking the colour rule altogether, by either going for white or for a rainbow. Both turned out to be impractical.

As Thierry recalled, "white was impractical, rainbow was too complicated, and then it was between petrol and pink. Pink was highly controversial—there were people who said, if it is pink, I am out of here. Some said, with pink we become the gay party, we can't do that. But we had the courage to go for it."

Emotions ran high when the group settled on pink. Some people did indeed leave the movement thereafter. But after some heated internal debates, the colour soon became a heavily endorsed symbol for NEOS—positive and progressive.

6.8   Cutting-Edge Communication

From the beginning, NEOS defined itself as a "Digital First" party. That was partly out of necessity: if you do not have access to public broadcasting, and pockets deep enough to invest in communication, you need to make the most of what you have at your disposal. For communication that means social media. But it was also a strategy. NEOS wanted to position itself as fresh and different. Back in 2012, traditional parties in Austria had yet to understand the potential of social media and its network effects. The first to understand this were the political parties on the right. Finding themselves insufficiently represented in "mainstream media", they started building their own "owned media" channels early on.

Things are different now, of course. The traditional parties have caught up. What Facebook images and Twitter posts were then, Instagram stories are now. What big databases were back then, behaviour-based CRM systems are now. For political start-ups, staying ahead of the game means recruiting the best communicators, and finding ways to make the most of their limited resources. It does not need an army; it needs a well-organised team to do cutting-edge communication.

Ciudadanos, for example, are very good at communicating. That dates back to their founding as an innovative Catalan citizen movement: "We say we were born in social networks" Carmen Cassa, then Head of Digital Communications, told me at the Ciudadanos headquarter in Madrid in June 2017. In the beginning, social media was an all-volunteers operation. "It was crazy back then, because it was a big team, we worked well and we won some prizes." But it was not sustainable. "Now we have professionals, and it's a small team—we have around 22 staff, and around 200 members working with them."

In 2017, they had three people on the strategy team and three more helping with content, videos and analysing social networks to monitor what was going on, and where people were talking about Ciudadanos. Under the strategy team, they had one staff member in every area in Spain, and volunteers working with them in every district.

Communicating in a consistent way can sometimes be a challenge, particularly with a crowd of 200 enthusiastic volunteers: "We don't want people... you know... using Photoshop and crazy pins. It was so hard to stop that, because everyone wants to help, and show their creativity. And sometimes it's the wrong design, or the wrong message" said Cassa. "But they take time out of their lives for us, so I think the key is to show them they are part of a big thing. It's very important to pay a lot of attention. We send them messages and when we go to different places, we try to have meetings with them. To sit in one place, have a beer, you know... we try to take care. And most weeks we spend with volunteers. We have some volunteers who create graphic material such as videos or images. They help us too. They spend a lot of time with us. And you know... with some of them I have a relationship, so if I see a book about politics I think they might like, I buy it; small things, details."

NEOS also focused early on "earned" media like Twitter, where you don't simply buy ads, but build your followers the hard way—by being interesting. What you get in return is quite direct and publicly observable access to opinion leaders, such as journalists and other influencers.

Focusing on social media, however, does not mean political start-ups should ignore traditional media. On the contrary. As Jorge Lobeto, at the time adviser to the Ciudadanos parliamentary group and now its communication manager, states dryly: "You go to small outlets, you go to small TV stations, you go to some freak programs, sometimes. But you break the barrier. You get the attention. And when you have the attention, you can build on it.. When it is a necessity, you don't choose it. It's all that you have. So you have to be good at it."

6.9   Reasoned Arguments

Peer review is a standard quality assurance procedure in science. Authors send draft papers and articles to a journal or a platform, where fellow academics scrutinise their content, style and structure. Most of the time, authors as well as the peer reviewers, are anonymous. There are reasons for that: personal relationships should not bias the judgement, and nor should fear of a backlash. After all, reputation is very important in science, and excessively harsh critiques might damage the reviewer just as much as the reviewed. The process is not without flaws: anonymity is at times just theoretical, particularly in niche scientific fields, where everyone knows each other. Sometimes, the reviewer might not have the specific expertise to appreciate the quality of a paper fully. And, as in all human affairs, vanity *does* play a role.

Recent innovations in this field have focused on opening up the rather closed process. Spearheaded by heavy hitters like the UK's Wellcome Trust, the "Open access" movement in science has created new platforms such as F1000Research. In contrast to traditional journals, F1000Research papers are available for free, and researchers can upload drafts and get qualified feedback from the scientific crowd.

There is nothing like that in traditional political parties. After all, politics is about power, and most power in democracies lies in the hands of the majority, not necessarily those with the best arguments. A new centrist politics that believes in the power of reason and empirical evidence must build structures and processes that not only allow for, but give weight and exposure to, reasoned arguments. That is evidence-based politics: basing policies on the best available knowledge, instead of relying merely on ideologies.

Debating policies at party conventions often leaves too little room for extensive and constructive scrutiny. Also, in most cases they reward physical presence—decisions are made by those attending. Drafting policies in small groups may be efficient, but it risks losing right of the viability of policies in the outside world.

Broad involvement of the public, however, can cost a lot of time and other resources and may lead to a considerable amount of frustration. What would processes and structures that efficiently consider a broad range of arguments, allow for information and consultation as well for managing expectations, look like?

The first political start-ups to experiment with tools to achieve these ends were the already mentioned Pirate parties that emerged across Europe around 2006, starting in Sweden, with their "liquid democracy" platform. Although technologically advanced, they were not very power-savvy and, with a few notable exceptions such as in Iceland, they crashed out of their parliaments in subsequent elections. The experiments continued, however. NEOS, for example, is operating an online platform called "Motion Forge", on which programme papers are reviewed and commented upon by members in a standard format. There are plans to develop Motion Forge into a genuine open innovation platform. Progressive Slovakia has built an open online forum, called "Komunita" where 2500 citizens and supporters regularly discuss policy issues (https://komunita.progresivne.sk/).

6.10   Looking Beyond National Borders

Twenty-first century political problems are not confined within national borders—so why should twenty-first century political parties be so confined? If the challenges we face are continental or even global, so should be the entities that address them.

In the short term, there is much to be learned from like-minded people in other countries. Just as young people provide fresh ideas and new approaches, so compatriots abroad are a valuable source of political innovation. Different countries do things differently, and sometimes very well. Living abroad, at least for a while, can make people even more committed and patriotic than stay-at-homers. Expatriates can also provide a political enterprise with a competitive edge, because traditional parties have not cared much for expats in the past.

Ludwig Grœsser was 23 studying marketing in Montreal at the time En Marche was established. Of 67 million French people, 3.3 million live abroad at any one time. In Montreal alone, there are 100,000 French citizens, 70,000 of whom are eligible to vote in French elections. Ludwig campaigned tirelessly, 5508 kilometres and one ocean away from Paris. In the end, 40% of French expatriates voted. They played a crucial role in Macron's success in the first round of the presidential election. Today, En Marche has 25,000 members abroad. Of the 11 seats in the Assemblée Nationale reserved for French people residing outside France, nine are from En Marche.

Austrian law does not yet provide for representation of Austrians abroad in the national Parliament. This is something NEOS calls for in its manifesto on democratic innovation. Just as in France, about 5% of the Austrian population resides outside the country. For the moment, NEOS sets a good example by providing Austrians abroad with a representative on its Extended Board, the highest strategic authority of NEOS. Austria has nine states, NEOS includes the rest of the world as a "10th state", and has an organisation, NEOS X, organised by expatriates.

That this is not about vanity or gadgetry, but about competitive advantage, is demonstrated by NEOS's history. The first ever information evening on NEOS, with the first draft manifestos fresh from the printing press, was held not in Vienna, but in a London pub. As I was living there at the time, I helped organise the evening with my colleagues Veit Dengler and Stefan Windberger, who managed to lure members of the Austrian Society at the London School of Economics. They fired salvos of policy questions at us, which we were barely able to answer satisfactorily. It was the first of many information evenings around the world. Together, they were one of the success factors of the NEOS project.

6.11 Resilience

As the African proverb has it: "If you want to go fast, go alone—if you want to go far, go together". Political start-ups can be initiated with the push of a button, or with a step-by-step process.

Initiating with the push of a button is much quicker, but it requires access to broadcasting and/or large-scale funding. Building a political start-up step-by-step, out of necessity or on purpose, takes longer, and requires more steps. It does, however, rely on fewer preconditions. Also, a longer process provides more scope for co-designing—involving stakeholders in the design process of the political start-up before its founding, to help ensure the result meets their needs and is practicable.

NEOS adopted the step-by-step approach to the organisational structure and the core policy programme in the belief that it would produce a more resilient organisation.

Resilience can also be enhanced by self-imposed rules for slower organic growth. For example, NEOS does not accept party switchers in parliaments. In the run-up to the 2013, election, a few representatives of other parties approached NEOS to gauge our in interest in them switching parties. NEOS's response was that if they wanted to join the party, they would have to go through the open primaries process. Almost all of them declined the offer. The comparison with Team Stronach, which also entered the Austrian Parliament in 2013, shows that politics by acquisition doesn't work.

They accepted sitting MPs from various parties, but Team Stronach disintegrated before the end of their first parliamentary term.

One key contribution political entrepreneurs can make to a start-up's resilience applies equally to business and social start-ups: try to make yourselves redundant. In other words, fill the leadership pipeline by hiring great people and empowering them to become the next generation of political entrepreneurs. Relying on one person to sort everything out is a recipe for disaster in the medium term.

Getting Competitive

Emmanuel Macron announced the launch of "En Marche" in April, 2016. He used his public platform as France's economy minister as a megaphone. One month later, the big reach-out and learning exercise "La Grande Marche" started. From May to June 2016, En Marche activists knocked at hundreds of thousands of doors all over France.

Supported by the consultancy Liegey Muller Pons (LMP), which had learned from the experiences of the campaigns of Barrack Obama in the US and François Hollande in France in 2012, En Marche systematically recorded the information gathered with a type-form available as a mobile app. The mountain of information was then analysed with the help of an algorithm. The results were shared in November, 2016 with the working groups that drafted the first version of En Marche's policy programme. Some measures proposed by citizens were included in the political programme and tested with focus groups.

During December, 2016 and February, 2017 Macron gave several topical speeches in which he included ideas gathered through La Grande Marche on such issues as education and the European Union. En Marche asked the 4000 local committees to organise debates and discussions after the speeches, to reflect the speech, and to provide new ideas for the programme in turn.

"There were thousands of these local events", according to Sandro Martin, one of the co-ordinators. The format was free, but again En Marche provided a pre-formatted typeform, a tool on the internet, to ask questions and collect the information. It was a structured process of iterative feed-back loops between citizens and En Marche members. In this way, the political enterprise validated and crowdsourced its policy platform and, at the same time, used the process to build up momentum, by continuously recruiting members and mobilising activists.

NEOS did something similar in 2012. Following the first assembly in February, the group instituted monthly general assemblies, designed as participatory citizen assemblies and open spaces. With every meeting, the group grew bigger. Five policy task forces were created to co-design the central policy areas: Democracy,

© Springer Nature Switzerland AG 2019
J. Lentsch, *Political Entrepreneurship*,
https://doi.org/10.1007/978-3-030-02861-9_7

Education, Economy, Europe and Social policy. Once the drafts were in, large citizen forums were organised in all nine states from June, 2012, under the brand of "Austria Speaks". This was based on the now defunct "America Speaks" format and was before NEOS had been promoted as a brand. The feed-back and ideas were woven into the policy drafts. In this way, "Austria Speaks" became the launch platform for NEOS.

In start-up terms, both En Marche and NEOS built prototypes of "minimum viable products" (in this case, policy papers). These prototypes were then road-tested with potential voters. The insights from their reactions and feed-back were translated into lessons that were validated by qualitative and, in En Marche's case, quantitative data. In the light of these outcomes, the policy papers were revised, and the learning loop started again.

Momentum used this basic model in Hungary, in 2015: every quarter, they had an open camp open to anyone who was interested. "Summer house-ish", Katka Cseh, one of Momentum's founding members, called it. "First, it was around 50 participants, then about 100. All of them were very active, getting to know each other more, talking about politics, agreeing on the statutes of the organisation. Then we founded the Momentum association, and registered it. . . we invited experts, political scientists, social scientists, to give talks and run seminars; everything mixed together over 4 days." They set up seven working groups at the camps, to work on core areas of the manifesto.

7.1   Critical Mass

What if there is no critical mass of already mobilised citizens, as there was for Nowoczesna in Poland in 2015, to tap into? What if one does not command a public platform as Emmanuel Macron did as serving Minister of Economics, or Yair Lapid did as one of Israel's best-known news anchors? How can one build a movement, when its public platform needs to be built at the same time?

Access to broadcasting is critical to the success of political start-ups, as Nicole Bolleyer showed in her seminal study "New Parties in Old Party Systems" (op. cit.). Although the tide may be turning—social media has re-written the rules of one-to-many communication—printed newspapers and TV, in particular, still play a powerful role in deciding whose political voices are heard. Political start-ups often lack the funds to buy access to these traditional media, particularly before an election campaign. If they cannot buy advertising space, they need to find other ways to get coverage. That's another entrepreneurial challenge.

"We did not know how we could raise our flag in Hungarian politics", András Fekete-Győr, founder of Hungary's Momentum movement told me, as he looked back to 2016. One-year-old Momentum had already decided to run candidates in the next parliamentary elections in 2018. But that was 2 years away. How could they, as a young, extra-parliamentary movement, with 143 members, gain traction and become a political power player in Hungary?

"We felt we had already done so many things in our organisation that were good. But it was *l'art pour l'art* [art, for art's sake]. People did not know about us" said Fekete-Győr. Until. . .

A Momentum member reported on Facebook that the right-wing FIDESZ government of Viktor Orbán planned to apply to host the 2024 Olympic Games in Budapest. According to polls, Hungarian society was split on the issue, but the government was only putting one-side of the argument. They really wanted to get the Games, for political communication and "national pride" reasons. So Momentum members came up with the idea of calling for a referendum on the application.

"We were a bit afraid", Fekete-Győr told me. "I, as President, asked myself 'is this a good idea?' We were not sure this was the right topic. But then you are always afraid when you go public, and show yourself. We are all more comfortable in our own caves."

They decided to go ahead with the referendum process on December, 2016. As the Olympic Games would take place exclusively in Budapest, a successful referendum in the capital would be enough to kill the application process. The magical number was 138,000 valid signatures, or 10% of registered voters. Suddenly Momentum people were all enthusiastic: now they had a project that seemed doable, with the potential to thrust them into the national political spotlight.

The first challenge was to get a court to accept a referendum question. They found out, to their astonishment, that someone had already successfully submitted a question, but had done nothing about it. So Momentum went with exactly the same question, which the court, having already approved it once, could not refuse. The FIDESZ government was taken by surprise.

Momentum had 3 weeks for preparations around Christmas: communication, logistics, recruiting of activists, fundraising—all at the same time. "We did our best, and that was very exciting" said Fekete-Győr. On the first day, in the freezing cold, Momentum activists collected 10,000 signatures.

A few weeks later, the project was already a topic of university courses, and on the street. After all, most of the liberal youth of Hungary lived in Budapest.

The young outsiders who came from nowhere to challenge the mighty Viktor Orbán also made for good copy. Images of people queuing to sign the referendum made the front pages. Was Momentum really founded only a year earlier? Who were they? What else did they want? Momentum used the public attention to present itself and its broader policy platform.

The propaganda media started to attack Momentum. To half of the population, it was like Goliath assaulting David: on one side the autocratic government machine, on the other young, democratic, likable citizens. At one point, the Government branded Momentum as "national traitors". Orbán personally called them "murderers, dream killers." The tactic back-fired and mobilised civil society even more. "So the people were saying, like, 'what the hell is the Government doing?'" Fekete-Győr recalled.

FIDESZ changed tack five or six times, but found no effective strategy. They wanted to avoid arguments with Momentum, but at the same time they couldn't ignore it. In the meantime, Momentum kept campaigning on the streets of Budapest saying "We do not want a basketball stadium, we want well-developed hospitals, and a good schooling system."

They had 30 days for the collection of signatures. Instead of the required 138,000 signatures, they collected 266,000. The Olympic application was dead. Momentum had managed to deal FIDESZ a telling blow, by channelling discontent with the government. "When I announced the result on February 27, all Hungarian media were there, and international media also", said Fekete-Győr. He found himself on the front pages of the main Singaporean newspaper, and on the radio in Southern France. The government was shocked, and cancelled the referendum. During the referendum it was Momentum's policy not to accept new members, according to Katka Cseh, one of the organisers, to avoid being infiltrated. Now applications for Momentum membership started to pour in by the thousands.

Immediately after handing over the 266,000 signatures, Momentum went on a 45-day-long roadshow across Hungary. They had such full houses that people were queuing to get in. Thus the roadshow became the basis for Momentum's nationwide organisation.

Similarly, Nowoczesna went on a tour across Poland following its sensational first convention with 8000 participants in Warsaw. The plan was to visit the 20 largest cities. And again big crowds showed up: 500 in Krakow, 700 in Wroclaw, 1200 in Poznan. They used the events to establish local structures, and recruited between five and ten people per city, to form the core teams of the local branches.

Summer intervened, however. "Summer time polls went down, because people were not interested in politics then. And it was a very hot summer, 37 degrees. People stopped believing us," Nowoczesna founder, Ryszard Petru, told me at the ALDE Congress in Amsterdam. Nowoczesna's first congress had caught the government off-guard. This time, the government was better prepared. Public broadcasting began to ignore Nowoczesna, and the party plunged in polls to 1%. "It was the most difficult summer in my entire career", said Petru.

But Nowoczesna kept going.

Progressive Slovakia is the youngest political start-up of the seven I describe in this book. At the time of writing in August, 2018, they were polling at 4.2%, above the threshold of the 4% required to enter Parliament. When I talked to their co-founder, Ivan Stefunko on Skype, in April, 2018, he told me of the structured strategy they adopted to go from nothing, to being a serious contender in less than 2 years.

The first step was creating a think-tank, in the form of a civic organisation, on which to build an organisational platform. There were ten founding members (most of whom went on to become members of the party Board). The plan was to see whether they could transform the think-tank into a full-blown party. For that, they had five pre-requisites:

Pre-Requisites for the Birth of a New Party
An ideologically compatible group: "Not necessarily exactly the same" said Stefunko, "but compatible. Not socialist authoritarian, like SMER, or conservative, or libertarian—we defined ourselves as liberal in terms of civil liberties, but near the centre economically. In left and right-logic: centrist." They recruited an initial 150 supporters.

Finance for the start-up: They found five entrepreneurs, including Stefunko himself, who each committed €200,000. In addition, they started crowdfunding early on.

Get media attention, and sound out public reaction: "We organised a meeting with intellectuals and journalists, and presented to them. We told them we wanted to implement this think tank project and, if it worked, we wanted to transform it into a political movement" Stefunko explained. The reaction was positive, so they carried on.

Build up critical mass: "We launched an online platform, 'Komunita', to discuss several political topics (https://komunita.progresivne.sk/). It was and is very successful. About 2500 people are active participants in Komunita discussions."

Road-test and reiterate: "The last thing we wanted to do was to travel around Slovakia" Stefunko continued. "We identified 13 cities, and then we added Brussels, Prague and Brno and other cities where lots of Slovaks were living. In each city we presented our vision, and facilitated a discussion with the people. The rooms were full, and people were really engaged. We felt a real groundswell of demand for a new kind of politics."

Once they had met all the pre-requisites, they decided to move on to the next phase in February, 2017. They invited more than 100 people to a cottage in central Slovakia, where the decision was taken to launch the process of registering the party. In Slovakia, 10,000 signatures are required by law to create a political party. Many parties do that, by paying young people a small sum to sign, but Progresívne did it themselves. The party was launched in January, 2018.

7.2 Found/Launch

Back then, the likelihood of failure was so huge [laughs.] and the likelihood of success so small. . . it was easy for us to get going with a certain light headed 'what the hell"-mentality.
Beate Meinl-Reisinger (in conversation, January 2018)

It was a cold, snowy day in January, 2018, when I drove 277 kilometres from Vienna to Žilina in Slovakia. I was accompanied by Stefan Windberger, the International Officer of NEOS. We were heading for an historic event. A centrist political start-up called "Progresívne Slovensko" (Progressive Slovakia) would establish itself that day. The formalities would be conducted during the day; celebratory speeches and a party would follow in the evening. It was no accident that the launch did not take place in Bratislava, Slovakia's capital. Žilina was the seat of Slovakia's first government until 1919. Today, it is Slovakia's fourth largest city, and an important industrial centre in the Northwest of the country, close to both the Czech and the Polish borders.

After driving for 3 hours through snow-covered flatlands and hills, we arrived in an industrial area. We waded through the slush of the parking lot, and entered a dark stylish hall. Inside, there were about 500 mostly young people. I estimated the average age to be 35. The event was well organised. In addition to the audience seated theatre-style, there were three rows of seats behind the stage, reserved for young activists. Everything was bathed in blue, red and purple, Progresívne's signature colours. A young Slovak called Peter checked us in. "Normally I am in Luxembourg, working at the European Court of Justice" he told us. "I am just here for this."

We were seated in the front row. The speeches and discussions were in Slovak, but a Progresívne volunteer sat down next to me, and translated simultaneously in flawless English. The lights went down, and a well-known Slovak stand-up comedian, who had been hired as the moderator of the evening, opened proceedings. After a few jokes and a description of the schedule, he handed over to Ivan Stefunko, the founder of Progresívne.

Stefunko talked passionately about the need for Slovakia to progress. He said it was the reason the party had been founded and named Progresívne.

"We have one goal", he said, "to move Slovakia forward. No one else can do it for us. We need better schools, and healthcare at European standards. We are here to bring about major changes. At the moment, those who thrive have money, power or luck. We have a different idea of progress—everyone should live up to their potential.... Now is the time to make our schools better, make it easier for entrepreneurs. Justice available for everyone!" He was interrupted several times by loud applause. The sense of excitement was palpable.

Stefunko's speech was followed by inspirational talks by citizens, activists, celebrities, and Progresívne parliamentary candidates. Progresívne had already recruited 750 volunteers. Two of them were interviewed on-stage. Bibiana was 19 and studying to become a teacher. She wanted to work with disabled children. "Stefunko talked about education, and I liked that", she said. Boris ran a co-working space in Košice. "I left Slovakia 2 years ago. Then I came back and started the co-working space. When the Progress tour hit town, I liked them so much, I joined."

Next came Matúš Vallo, an architect who was running as the Progresívne candidate for Mayor of Bratislava. He talked about how cities change the way we live our lives, and presented case studies of urban renewal, all incorporated in a city strategy called "Plan B" (B for Bratislava). He showed pictures of how he and his team had already started to make a difference in the capital—a bus stop they made more attractive, a market hall they re-purposed and a local festival that connected the white and Roma populations.

Michal Šimečka, a political scientist and Progresívne's International Officer, talked about Europe, and the value the EU provide for citizens. He talked of two identities—the Slovak and the European, which he said could co-exist. "If we want progressive Slovakia, we need to fight for a progressive Europe as well."

Zora Jaurova, a producer and dramatist, who had just stepped down from her role as President of the Creative Industry Forum Slovakia, talked about culture: "Culture is the largest economic value in the world right now" she said. "It is a part of everything that we are, and it goes where it can develop freely." She advocated beauty in politics and in justice.

Lawyer, Zuzana Caputova, talked about justice and consumer rights: "We feel the balance if something is right or wrong. In Slovakia, this balance is damaged. We want to bring back fairness, honesty and justice to the country."

Finally, Michal Truban, a 34-year old technology entrepreneur and investor, and a co-founder of Progresívne, compared entrepreneurship with politics. "What is the difference between them?" he asked rhetorically. "In entrepreneurship, you have 50% under control; in politics, only 10%."

The speeches made clear that Progresívne was a broad church of progressive people in the political centre: environmentalists, social justice advocates, consumer rights activists, entrepreneurs, Europhiles, and others. What had brought them together was a hope for a better tomorrow, a fairer society, a stronger economy and a more open democracy. The depth of the Slovak political crisis became apparent only a few months later, when the 27-year old investigative journalist Ján Kuciak and his fianceé Martina Kušnírová were murdered. This led to the resignation of Prime Minister Robert Fico.

Another kind of political crisis brought Spanish Ciudadanos into existence. As José Manuel Villegas, now Member of the Spanish Parliament, recounted when I visited the offices of the Parliamentary group of Ciudadanos in Summer 2017. The movement that would form the base for the liberal political start-up Ciudadanos was launched in Catalonia with a manifesto.

"In the beginning there was a manifesto, signed by 15 very well-known intellectuals in Catalan society; people from the arts, philosophy, etc. The manifesto was widely publicised in the media, and the internet—we didn't have social media then. It was very successful, and people could join the movement created by that manifesto. In a few months about 3000 people in Catalonia signed up to the movement. A civil association, not a political party, was created first. Between June 2005 and July 2006, the movement and the association organised events throughout Catalonia. And we realised there really was a good base, and a need for this political party."

This manifesto was entitled "Primer Manifest de Ciutadans de Catalonia" (First Manifesto of Citizens of Catalonia). Ciutadans later also became the party name.

The movement's pillars, as stated in the manifesto, were:

- Citizenship
- Liberty and Equality
- Secularism

- Bilingualism
- Constitution

As an interesting post-script, just before the formal creation of the party, the 15 intellectuals announced that none of them would join the new party. "They realised the party was necessary, but they didn't see themselves as integral parts of it", Villegas, who was a member of the first steering committee of the association before Ciudadanos in 2005, told me. They became midwives of the new party, not its creators.

Celebrities help a new movement get media attention, and propel it into the public eye. Often, however, political entrepreneurs will not have access to well-known personalities. In many cases, even if they have sympathies, they will not want to expose themselves as supporters of a potentially unsuccessful start-up. That may ultimately turn out to be a good thing: relying too much on celebrities can be a curse for political start-ups, as Guillaume Liegey, partner of the consultancy LMP has often observed in France:

"We wanted to launch the movement [En Marche] long before the election" he said. "We could not just count on media attention. A few other political movements that were started in France failed because they didn't realise that media attention doesn't last. It is not enough to structure something in the long run. If you want to structure a movement in the long run, and keep it alive, you need real people to do real stuff, and meet together to do stuff. That is a necessary condition. If you don't do that, and just count on the fact that your leaders appear on TV, maybe it's gonna last a few months, but then it is going to collapse."

That's exactly what happened to Team Stronach, the populist party start-up of Austrian billionaire, Frank Stronach, in 2013. Stronach was one of the best known business personalities in Austria. That certainly helped with the media at the beginning. Team Stronach successfully entered parliament with 5.7% of the vote on its first attempt, attaining a slightly better result than NEOS, the other newcomer. But it quickly became apparent that the party was him and him alone; that his parliamentary group was full of political mercenaries and soldiers of fortune, and that they had no idea how to build, much less how to scale, a movement. Team Stronach soon crashed in the polls, lost its MPs one by one, and did not survive its first term in parliament.

NEOS held its founding convention on 27 October 2012, the day after the Austrian National Day. Some 250 people attended the event at the Urania, a public educational institute and observatory. The room was packed, and the atmosphere joyful. Matthias Strolz was elected Chairman, and alongside him were an 11-strong Board, myself among them. Strolz made a speech that can still be found on YouTube. Six years later, it still holds up well. On this day, NEOS became the pro-European, pro-market, progressive liberal political start-up, with the ambition of transforming the Republic with "new faces, a new style and new politics", as the flyers on the tables stated.

En Marche took a meticulous approach to preparing the launch that ultimately took place on April 6, 2016.

The first meeting of what would become En Marche occurred in Summer, 2015, recalled Guillaume Liegey. He had participated in the Obama campaigns of 2008 and 2012, and had helped Francois Hollande win the Presidency. Liegey had known Emmanuel Macron for a few years, from when he had been a civil servant. They assembled a small working group of trusted advisors and professionals who were ready to volunteer their expertise as accomplices. At one of their dinners, Liegey said for the first time: "So, if you want to become President, you have to do the following. . .".

Together, they looked at what had worked in the past, and what had not: "We took benchmarks of a lot of failed attempts to create new parties, to understand what didn't work with them, and to learn from their mistakes.

And then", Liegey explained, during our interview on Skype, "we tried to anticipate what would happen when he announced his intention to run. I think the problem they had was that they would have to appear very innovative. They wanted to use the launch of the movement to change Macron's image. Macron's image was that of a liberal, elitist guy, who was an investment banker, and who was very close to very wealthy people in Paris—that was the perceived Macron. So they said, whatever we do when we launch the movement, we need to change that."

The other thing was that they wanted to launch the movement long before the election. They did not just want to rely on media attention. A few other political movements that had been started in France failed exactly because of that: they didn't realise that initial media attention doesn't last (see above).

They decided on three main criteria for framing the launch of En Marche. First, project a different image of Macron. Prove that Macron could be closer to the people, and could do politics in a different way. That had to be Macron's overarching message: I want to do politics differently. Second, they wanted something that would last; something that wouldn't rely entirely on media attention. Third, it would be a very new movement. If eventually they ran a presidential campaign, they would need to be ready from the start. So launching the movement 1 year before the elections was a good opportunity to get in some practice.

Macron wanted to do politics differently. At the same time he realised that once you run for President, *every* meeting is biased. People know you are a candidate, and there are media around you all the time. He felt caught in an ivory tower, and people perceived him to be elitist. How could he change that?

This was where the idea of societal stakeholders came in. One idea was to collect conversations with citizens. As a candidate, Macron would not have the time to meet 25,000 people in person. But the movement could conduct and record those conversations for him. That would give him and En Marche a window into the daily lives of those people.

7.3   The Story of La Grande Marche

Liegey and his colleagues looked at the most innovative recent campaigns, such as Obama's in 2008 and 2012, and how they combined data, technology, people and direct contact to organise a massive "get out the vote" effort, with lots of door-to-door activities. At the end of December, 2015, they came up with the idea of "La Grande Marche", a large-scale, nationwide door-to-door campaign that would kick off immediately after the launch of En Marche.

But there were doubts within the small working group, Liegey remembered: "They said, you know, 'Why door-to-door? What are we going to say 1 year before the elections? It doesn't make sense to say "Vote for Macron", because he will not be a candidate at the time. And also, we will be a young movement, so we will not have many people.'"

Liegey recalled passionately advocating in favour of La Grande Marche, and arguing why it made sense exactly at a time where there was no election looming: "Something that has never been done is using door-to-door, not to try to persuade people, but to *listen* to them. This is an idea Arthur Muller, Vincent Pons (his two partners at LMP) and I had a long, long time ago for Hollande's campaign. After that campaign, we wrote a book, 'Porte-a-porte' (Door-to-Door), and at the end of the book, in the conclusion, we wrote what could be the lessons of this campaign for governing. We wrote, when you govern, it is important to maintain a relationship with the people. And we proposed this idea of using door-to-door as a way of keeping relationships with local people."

The group realised they could use La Grande Marche for building relationships as well as asking questions. The questionnaire comprised eight open questions:

- If you had a wish about politics, what would it be? (be concrete)
- Tell us of a concrete initiative in your neighbourhood that you want people to know about, and you want to strengthen?
- In your opinion, what works well in France?
- And what doesn't work?
- What is the best experience you have had since 2015?
- And what is the worst?
- What worries you about your personal future?
- What is your most important reason to be hopeful about your personal future?

This was followed by questions about the person's demographic background, and whether he or she wanted to stay in touch with En Marche, or perhaps even join.

Armed with all this information, they could do a technology-assisted diagnostic of the country. They would use the insights from talking to many stakeholders, and they wouldn't do politics the way it has always been done—writing policies behind closed doors without any input from the public.

"Something very important about La Grande Marche", Liegey emphasised, "was that it was not participative democracy. The idea wasn't to crowdsource the programme; not at all. There were no policy questions such as: 'if you were to change the country, which would be your top three policy measures?'. There was nothing like that, because it is completely unrealistic to expect to get smart answers when you just knock at somebody's door. The idea was really to listen to people, and then to use the results to force policy experts, who tend to work in closed rooms, to have a view on the outside world."

When they decided, in January, 2016, that this would be the main action after the launch, questions arose about how to plan it ahead of the launch. All the meetings of the small working group were highly confidential. Amazingly, the group Liegey was a part of never leaked. There were many press articles about Macron and reports that he was planning something, but they were not informed by people who were in the know. It was just people talking.

It was clear that, for La Grande Marche to be a success, the recruitment of field organisers—early follower volunteers who manage teams of volunteers—would be crucial. "It's really hard to find those people" Liegey told me when we discussed early followers. "You need people with a little bit of campaign experience. The problem was, due to confidentiality, we could not call anyone and say 'hey, we are about to start this operation'. But if we called them right after the launch, we would have found it hard to make the operation work, because time constraints were very tight."

The launch was scheduled for April 6. They decided training would begin only 10 days later. And then there would be training sessions for field organisers every Saturday until the end of May. They knew that, by the end of July, the operation had to be finished. People went on holiday then, and politics was not on their minds."We needed to organise a very well-structured, targeted campaign—without any party, without any database to work with, and without the ability to contact people we knew before the launch, because of the confidentiality" Liegey explained.

They planned what would happen on a day-by-day basis, before and after the launch. They asked everyone in the small group to contribute a list of at least five names they knew. From scratch, they built a list of about 100 people they could potentially call when Macron announced the launch of En Marche—without any guarantee that they would accept. For the first meeting, they had to have a full room, to get the dynamic going; beginnings matter. They needed a motivated group of field organisers to start recruiting and training volunteers, so that they could start to go out in the field.

They convinced En Marche to put a strong focus on La Grande Marche, to provide support for all the organisers.

"You can buy the best campaign software in the world—but if people do not use it, you have nothing", Liegey said. "And for people to use it, we knew, from our experience from the Hollande campaign, that once people start going out in the field, they will have questions. Sometimes it will be the software that doesn't work, sometimes they will struggle to recruit volunteers, sometimes they will challenge the given questions . . . lots of other questions we won't even be able to anticipate."

To make the campaign successful, they wanted to put together a team who could provide answers to field organisers and volunteers in less than 24 h. "Because if people ask questions and you don't answer them, they lose interest. This support team consisted of the equivalent of 10 full-time people, most of them students. They also recruited Stanislas Guerini to be a full time Project Lead for La Grande Marche. He is now an MP and the Deputy Whip in the Parliament."

In the end, they trained around 500 field organisers, and 6000 people participated in La Grande Marche. The project became the basis of the success story that would become Emmanuel Macron and En Marche.

Back then, however, not even the activists themselves believed Macron had a chance of winning the Presidency.

"I remember, we were doing decision trees with some colleagues: what are the chances of even running without a socialist candidate, let alone winning? Our calculations resulted in a chance of pretty much zero" Sandro Martin, who was working as field organiser in the 11th arrondissement of Paris, told me.

"Mobilising people to do things for you for free is one of the hardest things in the world," Liegey states dryly. So why did they do it?

"I don't think people joined En Marche in the beginning because they thought Macron would be elected; I think they joined because they enjoyed doing what they did. For me, it was very enjoyable, even though it killed my personal life for 9 months.

From my perspective, I have had discussions with every political entrepreneur in France over the past 5 years. At some point any people who were serious about starting something new contacted our company, LMP. The En Marche people were the best I saw. They were really much better on so many levels, they were much more professional, they were nicer in a way. It was a pleasure to work with them. They are all like in the series *The West Wing*. Of course it was tough, and Macron is a tough guy. He is a really tough manager, and very demanding. But I really enjoyed it."

Ready, Steady, Go

8

JL: "So, back to 2015. You were on the campaign, you did it all at once, you freestyled. What were the challenges you faced?"

Miłosz Hodun (Nowoczesna): "Everything!"

Once the founding is done and basics, including a solid core group, a manifesto, and a party constitution, are in place, political start-ups need to get competitive, fast. That is easier written than done, of course, because, as in business, "competitiveness" in the political arena is multi-faceted.

If you do only one thing, however, *attract good people*. Voters are influenced most by people. Politics is not traditionally associated with an abundance of talent. "The social perception of being a politician is really negative", said Begoña Villacís, the Speaker of Ciudadanos Madrid—and it's the same in almost every country. But that people such as Villacís, a highly successful corporate lawyer, who in her previous life had more than 50 lawyers working for her, make the decision to enter politics, shows that political start-ups, such as Ciudadanos, are starting to make a difference.

And that is part of the answer to how you attract talent to politics. "You can only attract interesting people as candidates if you have interesting people at the top; people with good ideas" said Veit Dengler, the first Managing Director of NEOS, who had previously managed 2000 people as General Manager of Dell. This implies that the greater the talent of the first generation of a political start-up, the greater the chances of attracting additional talent. While this is a precondition, however, it is no guarantee. Focusing on it means spending a lot of time meeting and evaluating potential candidates.

En Marche has taken that a step further. People interested in being candidates have to apply with their CV and a motivation letter, just as they would do for any other job. There are also procedural "filters" that can be used to separate the wheat

© Springer Nature Switzerland AG 2019
J. Lentsch, *Political Entrepreneurship*,
https://doi.org/10.1007/978-3-030-02861-9_8

from the chaff. The "open" primaries used by NEOS are a way to identify people who can campaign.

The exposure open primaries provide, however, can also be a challenge. Celebrities in particular may be unwilling to endure the hassle, and the risk of embarrassment if they don't get a good result. Also, it may be tactically smart to present a celebrity late in the game. For these reasons, the NEOS member assembly has also instituted an exception to the rule that everyone must do open primaries—the Extended Board may award one "Carte Blanche" to any position on the candidate list apart from the first. In 2017, this Carte Blanche went to Irmgard Griss, the former independent Presidential candidate.

Hire Key Staff

Another high priority is to hire a few key people to run the operation professionally. For candidates to be comfortable campaigning, they need to be sure HQ has their backs. A lot of areas can be covered with volunteers, but key functions such as organisation and communications need to be looked after by high calibre staff, 24/7.

Great people tend to be expensive, and money is a resource many political start-ups lack. Fortunately, as with social start-ups, it is amazing what people will sacrifice for idealistic reasons. A convincing political mission, and being part of a potentially historic initiative, goes a long way towards compensating people for cuts in salary.

As with candidates, hiring great people takes time, effort and creativity. It is essential, however. As in business, the rule is "A people hire A people". This sometimes means daring to say *no* to an available, but inadequate, candidate and holding out for someone better.

Shift Funding into a Higher Gear

"I remember how around January 14, 2012, I personally collected the first cheque for €10,000 in Vorarlberg, and how I delivered it to the bank", Veit Dengler recalled during our interview. "And I thought, great, now we can pay salaries—for January." Starting to hire as a political start-up means starting to sweat towards the end of the month: will we be able to pay our staff?

Crowdfunding is becoming more of a standard tool for campaigns these days—in 2012/2013, NEOS was one of the first European parties to crowdfund a large chunk of its campaign. But there is still a need for major donors, and bank loans. In the case of NEOS, the former came with the electoral platform through the Liberal Forum. Major donors were also offered a deal where they could grant a loan that would convert into a donation if NEOS didn't get into parliament.

In 2015 Nowoczesna only had 6 months to raise funds, between its founding and the next election, but it became the first Polish party to crowdfund its way into the Sejm, the lower house of Poland's Parliament. It managed to raise zł 11 Million (€2.6 Million). A tenth of the campaign budget was raised through the internet. Ryszard Petru, Nowoczesna's founder, saw fundraising as one of his key responsibilities: "I was fundraising all the time. When I read that Al Gore spent only 40% of his time on it, I said I can do the same. And I was talking, talking, talking to people all the time, and since I was coming from business, I knew plenty of people from business. So wherever I went, whichever city I went to, I met with entrepreneurs, talked about the idea, and asked for money. To make it you need money to pay people. That's how it is. If you don't have money, you can't be professional. You can be professional in empowerment, you can be professional in the speeches, but not in the organisation."

En Marche also put a strong focus on fundraising from early on. As Guillaume Liegey recalled, "the fundraising effort was unprecedented. It played a crucial role in the success of En Marche. Everything I described could happen because they had the money to pay for it. They had money to pay us; money to hire very good people full-time, early on. They raised more than €12 million. Maybe nothing compared to American campaigns, but the next most successful fundraisers in French political history were Alain Juppe and Francois Fillon—they raised €3–4 million."

Load the Contacts Database

Most traditional parties are not good at managing their contacts. This is another opportunity for political start-ups. However, to make good use of those contacts, you have to have someone sitting in front of the screen who really understands strategic marketing.

Whether you collect contacts door-to-door like En Marche, through citizen forums like NEOS, or with a petition like Momentum: collect contacts everywhere. And organise them via a state-of-the-art Customer Relationship Management platform. Best not to start with Excel lists from the outset, because they tend to become permanent once set up.

Go on Tour

Political start-ups can spend weeks formulating strategy, and discussing internal matters. If they want to become competitive, however, they must go outside—ideally, with wind in their sails. After Momentum had defeated the Hungarian Government with their petition against the Olympic Games, they went on the road.

"Immediately after we handed over the 266,000 signatures, we went on a roadshow in Hungary" Andras Fekete-Győr told me. "And this was good. We went to cities. We had full houses. We had such large audiences, many people couldn't get into the venues. There were queues outside.

And it was very worrying for Fidesz—they are afraid of a party with a nationwide organisation. Right now we have a nationwide organisation. Of course, it can be even wider. But at the time we had this 45-day roadshow. And people were very, very excited about Momentum. 'Who are they?' people wondered. 'They have had this big success' with the NOlimpia thing [as the petition was called].

So half of the nation, meaning the Fidesz people, hated us. Because we were the dream murderers, the 'dream killers', as Viktor Orban called us."

What better public relations could you wish for?

Earn Media Coverage

Unless political start-ups have access to broadcasting via a celebrity or other contacts, they have to *earn* their media coverage. They have to try to get in direct contact with opinion formers. At the time of writing, Twitter, for example, is still a useful tool for that. To make it work, however, candidates need to understand how social media works, and the various organisational media accounts on Facebook, Twitter, Instagram, etc. need a full-time professional operating them.

Join Forces

One way to strengthen leverage, and to consolidate the market *before* the campaign kicks off, is to enter into strategic alliances with potential competitors, or non-competitors that have something crucial to add. Ideally, they complement the strategic assets of the start-up.

In the case of NEOS in 2013, the Liberal Forum had the network and the access to major donors, and the Young Liberals had troops on the ground. Stefan Egger, then a Liberal Forum sympathiser, remembered his personal epiphany: "I attended a so-called 'Federal Partners assembly', in the backroom of a coffee house, when the Liberal Forum was still quite small. I was then invited to a real partners' assembly at a hotel, where the actual decisions were made, and where Matthias Strolz made an appearance. I only went because I wanted to have the experience once. There was this bundle of energy jumping around the room, and suddenly this round came to life. And I thought, now is the time you should join the Liberal Forum." Egger would later become Parliamentary Group Director and then Executive Director of NEOS.

In 2017, NEOS also entered another alliance with Irmgard Griss, former chairwoman of the Supreme Court. She ran as an independent presidential candidate in 2016 and achieved 18.9% of the vote in the first ballot, missing the runoff by only a few points. She had the gravitas NEOS lacked, and electoral success, to boot.

Of course, those alliances create their own dynamics that need managing. But there is no prize for purity in politics. If an alliance makes sense for pragmatic reasons, there is a strong case for considering it.

Get a Rebel Base

Every political start-up needs a home-base to work, to socialise, to chill. It needs to be large enough to house a potentially quickly growing campaign team. After all, you do not want to switch or split offices right in the middle of the action. With the help of a supportive real-estate agent, NEOS rented an open space office on the top floor of an office building in the 7th district of Vienna in 2012. An internal competition led to it being christened the "Neosphere". It remains the NEOS home-base to this day.

8.1   Run

Grace Pardy had been a successful international strategic marketing executive at Coca-Cola, Dockers and Reebok. Early 2013, she was working in Sweden. Veit Dengler, then Executive Director of NEOS, got word that she was available. At the time, NEOS had a "spontaneous awareness" of 7% (the proportion of respondents who mentioned NEOS without being prompted). He knew that voters, who do not know you, will never vote for you. So he needed a campaign manager to help boost that within little over 6 months. The elections would be in September.

Veit introduced Pardy to NEOS via a "NEOS@home" evening, where people invite friends to their homes, to discuss politics with NEOS representatives in an informal and relaxed atmosphere. Afterwards, he introduced her to NEOS Chairman Matthias Strolz. They clicked, and started to talk about options. She was surprised because she had no traditional political campaigning experience. "This I cannot deliver. What I can deliver is what I know from my branding background; mobilising people for action, strategy, data and all that. And a more or less disruptive creative approach," she told them. "And if that is something you want, and you feel is going to lead to the one-liner briefings that get us into parliament in six months or so, then yes." Pardy started in April.

A Day in a Campaign
A conversation with Stefan Egger, managing director of NEOS

JL   When did the whole campaign take off?
SE   It started in March. From June it was "come in the morning, and never leave."
JL   What did a day look like?
SE   Utterly unplannable. There was an incredible amount of work, but there were few deadlines, which makes for absurd situations, and an unstructured to-do list that never ended. That changed after a while.

In August, the campaign became much more dynamic. We now had significantly more people; we developed structures and convened meetings. We had a lot of street events and activism.

The core team at the time were 15–20 people. The rest were volunteers, many of whom only joined in September. We became large only at the end, before that it was a small and rather crazy group.

I was always approachable, as I was always there.

In April 2013, the NEOS Board, with representatives of other partners on the electoral platform, the Liberal Forum and the Young Liberals, went on a retreat to the Loisium in Lower Austria. It was supported by the Alliance of Liberals and Democrats (ALDE) in Europe, the European party of which the Liberal Forum had already been a member. "So, where do you think we stand right now?" Philip Hansen, ALDE's Head of the Political Unit, asked. There was a lot of optimism in the room, a lot of ambition, and also some over-estimation of where they actually stood. In other words, the typical start-up enthusiasm.

They knew that to be successful they would need other people's money. A lot of it. "Probably in every country there is a minimum budget to become visible," Michael Bernhard, NEOS' financial officer explained when we talked. "Our marketing experts calculated this sum for Austria in 2013 to be €2–2.5 million. You need a base of professional staff, which you cannot cover with volunteers. On top of that there were marketing costs, of course."

While they knew their expenses would be €2–2.5 million, they did not know where that money would actually come from. The initial idea was for NEOS and the Liberal Forum to raise funds for the electoral platform on a half-and-half basis. "But we later departed from that" said Bernhard "when we saw that, what was back-then the NEOS side, contributed lots of voluntary work that would have cost lots of money, which we did not have. And there was also Hans-Peter Haselsteiner, who would not have invested in the Liberal Forum without NEOS."

Haselsteiner later signed a personal loan guarantee of €600,000 and donated another €600,000. "And we made a deal with the media", Bernhard explained, "which I would not do again, at least now that we are in Parliament. The deal involved a success premium. We agreed with Puls4, a private TV station, to run advertisements that we would only pay for if we entered parliament. If we got in, we would pay them out of our public subsidies and bank loans. The deal involved about €500,000, so with €600,000 plus €600,000 plus €500,000, we already had around €1.7 million."

In addition to this, there were lots of smaller, and some large donations, from around 1100 citizens, amounting in total to €655,000. No other party had raised that much money from crowdfunding in Austria.

Following the Loisium retreat, the Board's first task was to put an initial campaign team together. They found six people who Bernhard described as "very passionate, very good, and very energetic." The second task was to get quantitative research data, to contrast the warm feelings with hard facts. NEOS had to be successful across all regions of Austria, but its strongholds were Vienna in the East and Vorarlberg in the West. Also, as a political start-up, NEOS had to identify who its constituency were, to be able to target them. When the figures came out, they poured cold water on some of the more fanciful estimates. Only 7% of survey respondents stated spontaneously that they knew us. NEOS had a long way to go.

One way to go, Grace Pardy figured, was to go outside, and go big. After all, the expectations in the political and media circles were that NEOS was too small to make it. That was an assumption that had to be corrected. The idea we came up with was to rent the well-known and beautiful "Palmenhaus" (Palm house) in May in Vienna's city centre, and stage a large-scale festivity. Speakers would talk about ideas in the core areas of the NEOS manifesto, such as education, economy, welfare reform and democratic innovation. The first internal reaction was scepticism: "Can we really fill that space?" They decided to go for it and 400 people showed up. We ended up with some great media coverage, but more importantly, we managed to surprise others and ourselves.

The other way to go, Pardy proposed, was to go inside, and go small. The aim was to get into people's homes. NEOS already had a tried and tested format for that. Between March and September 2013, right up to the election on September 29, NEOS conducted more than 200 "NEOS@home" events in people's living rooms all over Austria. At first, they were somewhat self-mockingly called "Political Tupperware Parties", because we were metaphorically "selling" our candidates and our policies. We received a nice, but formal letter from Tupperware, asking us kindly to abstain from using their brand in a political context. Of course, we complied.

The "NEOS@home" format became a raging success. It arose, as is often the case with political start-ups, from frugal innovation. We did not have any money to organise expensive events. We also knew Austrians were not always comfortable debating politics in public, much less being associated with a political start-up most thought had zero chance of entering parliament.

This cultural unease dates back to the Biedermeier period in the first half of the nineteenth century, when Metternich ran an authoritarian surveillance state. The only place people felt secure enough to discuss public matters was in private. This led to the Viennese tradition of the Salon (with the French pronunciation). Back then, a usually upper-class host or hostess invited a small circle of people from society, such as authors, artists and businessmen, into his or her home. As in France, the Viennese Salons were idea hubs that became important for the cultural and intellectual development of society. They culminated in the revolutions of 1848 in the Austrian empire. Looking back, it seems logical that a civic movement, such as NEOS, which advocates bloodless political revolution, would employ a contemporary version of the time-honoured salon model.

The deal was simple: people would invite friends and friends of friends to their homes, and provide some drinks and nibbles. We would provide one of the leaders of NEOS, who would present our positions and discuss them with the group, based on a simple manual we provided them with. Sometimes there were 10 participants, sometimes 30 or more. We also used the Salons shamelessly to raise funds, by passing around the transparent donation box. The format has since been adopted in other countries, such as Germany.

Throughout the summer, Grace Pardy and the team also toured across Austria. "I think I toured Austria three times, to make sure that the regional teams were kept in the loop, engaged and got what they needed" she recalled.

NEOS also organised more than 150 "information evenings", publicly announced presentations, followed by audience Q&As, all over Austria.

To be eligible to contest an election NEOS had to collect signatures from citizens in all nine Austrian states. It is a formal procedure that takes time, and is tediously bureaucratic. So why not make it fun? "There is always something to being first" said Pardy. "So when we were ready to go, we said 'we can't go in with no goal'. So we set ourselves the goal of being the first party to get all the signatures. And that was so interesting to see. It sparked off an internal regional competition." Ultimately, NEOS came in as the first new party to collect all the required signatures.

Targets and Messages
Everything was based on data. The information was gathered through quantitative and qualitative research, such as focus groups, but also systemic constellation work, a therapeutic method to reveal a supposedly unrecognized systemic dynamic. It became apparent that the prime target groups were the young, the urban and the more educated.

The main line of attack was against the "standstill" of the Republic. Many citizens felt it viscerally, and wanted Austria to get moving again. The grand coalition of the Social Democrats and the Conservatives had dragged their feet on urgent reforms, and seemed to have no ambition other than to hold on to power. The attack would be creative, sometimes dramatic, but always authentic, and always in a positive and hopeful spirit—that things can be different, and better.

It was similar to Ciudadanos in 2015, as Jorge Lobeto told me: "Our main message was hope. This was unlike Podemos, who were playing the card of rage—'they're screwed up, they're screwing us, they've been screwing us for 40 years, it's time to kick them out, we're going to take heaven by the sword!' It was also unlike Partido Popular, who were playing the card of fear—'if you let Podemos win, if you let the left come, it's going to be a disaster!' That was their main message. For us it was hope—and I remember clearly our message. It was: 'We have hope. We believe things are going to get better.' That was very good; it worked."

Despite the many NEOS events in both public and in private, it became clear that the required awareness could not be reached without significant investment in airtime on mass media. So, Pardy negotiated a far-reaching deal with private TV and radio, sharing the financial risk with them. The combined efforts of Pardy, the campaign team and everyone else paid off: spontaneous awareness rose from 7% in April to 47% in September.

Last Minute Stunt

In the weeks before the election, according to internal figures, NEOS was polling at 3–3.5%, and rising. The threshold to enter the Austrian Parliament is 4%. "If you believed the trend would continue, then we were in—if you believed the trend would flatten somewhat, then we were not," Stefan Egger told me. "The biggest threat next to our obscurity was the 'lost vote'-problem". The "lost" or "wasted" vote-problem is a challenge faced by new as well as small parties: people want their vote to matter. If they are concerned that a particular party might not make it into Parliament, some of them will switch allegiance to another one that will. This can become a self-reinforcing vicious circle in the weeks ahead of the election. "It kills you when you are somewhere around the electoral threshold in the polls", Egger explains to me. "When you weaken towards the end, you're dead. And then we got Haselsteiner on board."

Hans-Peter Haselsteiner, one of Austria's most successful entrepreneurs, was a former MP for, as well as a long-standing supporter of, the Liberal Forum. "It was a conscious decision, to get that final 1%. We said we didn't want to risk it, and convinced him to announce that he would be ready to serve as a Minister, should NEOS get into Government. With this we secured our position: getting him to endorse us publicly as a highly reputable, well-known personality, and the funding that came with it. The media impact was the largest we had over the whole campaign."

The "Operation Steinadler" (Operation Golden Eagle), as it was called, almost failed before it started, when Haselsteiner found the codename to be stupid ("Which idiot came up with that?" he asked). In the end, the last minute Haselsteiner stunt helped NEOS to reach 4.96%, or 232,946 votes.

Conflicts

"Democracy happens before and after election campaigns. You gotta make tough decisions and you gotta stick with it," said a campaigner with lots of experience, Annelou van Egmond of the Dutch D66. This applies to even the most participatory political start-ups. You cannot be friends with everyone when you run campaigns. Emotions often run high, and what might only peripherally touch you in another situation may turn into melodrama under high stress.

NEOS also experienced internal conflicts early on in the campaign. Surely, a campaign without conflicts is a dead campaign, but "we spent too much energy internally that we should have projected externally" Veit Dengler thought, in hindsight. "During this early phase, successful start-ups I know of are more decisive, and better able to avoid or manage conflicts."

It would take NEOS a few more elections to learn from that experience. The next national campaign, in 2017, was prepared for and organised in a much more professional way.

Fundraising

Money matters. Political start-ups can achieve a great deal with the idealism and commitment of their volunteers, but there is a difference between playing in the regional league and in the Champions League. As Matthias Strolz of NEOS likes to quip: "You can't play Champions League barefooted." For the equipment and all the extras, you need cash.

From the very beginning in 2012, NEOS instilled a crowdfunding culture, by passing around at each event a plastic cube that was see-through, to reflect its transparency claims. Of the €1.2 million raised, NEOS managed to get about half from 3000 small donors. That was unprecedented in Austria in more ways than one. First, no party had ever crowdfunded itself into the Austrian Parliament (only a couple had done so in any European parliament). Second, only the Greens in the 1980s had managed to enter Parliament with less money, in very favourable circumstances, which tells you how much money there is in the Austrian political system. For new parties, the need to raise such sums is, of course, one of the main barriers to entry into the political market, which is why NEOS calls for halving public party funding in Austria, which has one of the most generous schemes in the world. What these figures also tell you, however, is that you also need major donors to support your political start-up. In the case of NEOS, half the €1.2 million raised came from large donors through loans as well as donations.

With En Marche, the fundraising effort was similarly unprecedented. "Every time we had a meeting, we said 'don't forget to give', because in France we always have this fear of asking for money. For the first time we had a movement that took talking about money for granted. From the beginning we told people 'we are a new movement, we don't have any money. The only way we'll survive, the only way we can stay independent, is to get money from you. We will take whatever you want to give'" Aziz François Ndiaye recalled.

"It played a crucial role in the success. What happened could only happen because they had the money to pay for it" Guillaume Liegey of LMP agreed. "They had money to pay us, money to hire very good people full-time, early on. They raised more than €12 million, by far and away the largest sum ever raised by a French political party. Christian Dargnat was in charge of fundraising. If you ask him what the magic trick is, he will tell you there is one, hard work. You have a list of people, you call them, you ask them to give money—if they say no, you stop asking. If they say yes, you ask them for more. And if they don't say anything, you keep asking them the question and harassing them until they say yes or no."

As with NEOS, about half of the total sum raised came from major donors. The rest came from crowdfunding.

The Magic Formula

"There is no magic wand for winning elections. It's really a mind-set thing." Liegey told me. "En Marche understand this. So does Ciudadanos. They are serious about doing things differently. It's about a mind-set of doers. Macron is a doer."

But if there is no magic formula, how much of a role does mere luck play? This was the question I asked Sandro Martin of En Marche. "I would say it is 100% luck, and 100% the work Macron did before and during the campaign. We took advantage of all the situations. Of course, all the planets were aligned. But also, we had the perfect candidate at the right time, and a campaign team that was really, really into doing things differently, into winning each and every vote. It was really a moment of collective enthusiasm."

Liegey agreed: "If you were to explain the success of En Marche: first, they were super lucky. Second, they were very professional with La Grande Marche, the fundraising and everything else, and they were in 'doing mode'. If you want to do politics differently, a change in mind-set is essential. En Marche is a good example of this. And of course Macron himself – you don't have many people like him. Third, a great group of people who were good at exploiting the momentum. The rest was a bit more traditional."

Grace Pardy, the former campaign manager of NEOS, believes if there is one decisive thing, it is organisational culture. "As Peter Drucker said, 'Culture eats strategy for breakfast'. Culture is the ultimate decisive factor for winning elections. Do you have your people engaged? Do they believe? Are they running their staff as their own little kingdoms, or are they seeing the importance of joining together, for one purpose and one cause? And from a cultural perspective, that is more complex in political organisations than businesses, because of the more complex structures."

The Final Days

What are the last days of campaigning before the election like for a political start-up?

"At the end, it was like we were running all the time" Stefan Egger said of the last days of the NEOS campaign in 2013. "During the day, work, work, work, distribute flyers, be on the street, schlepping to exhaustion... and being caught in this crazy energy bubble, not being able to switch off, pulling all-nighters."

Remembering his last days on the road campaigning for Emmanuel Macron, Aziz François Ndiaye agreed: "It was very stressful. We were stressed because we didn't know at all how things would go. We didn't have any benchmarks for ourselves. It was our first experience."

The Macron campaigners felt they had to stay focused on all of the elements. For example, they had worked hard on the overseas votes, because they were expected to vote overwhelmingly for Macron, and could make a very important marginal difference. They also continued with door-to-door, to mobilise suspected voters, as well as to convince those who were undecided. Because of the unusual nature of the election, more citizens than ever remained undecided right up until polling day.

"So we stayed focused until the last minute... the last minute... I remember five minutes before the end of the campaign, we were still in the field, knocking on doors" said Ndiaye. "Psychologically it was very important – we prepared people a long time before to go into the field at the last minute, to convince the last people, because each vote counted. That was to keep them focused and mobilised until the end. I mean it was very tight, but we were able to get those three or four points that made the difference. We really went to great lengths to get every last one."

Election Day
"The day of the elections we were quite hopeful. Because we had the feeling that we had done the job. We had done the job right. We hadn't missed anything," Aziz François Ndiaye told me.

But it wasn't over yet.

"On the day of the election, I went to see all the vote officials myself, to make sure that everything went right" Ndiaye recalled. "Because again, we were not prepared; we didn't have any experience handling an election day. All the papers had to be correct, so we didn't have any surprises. We had a special team we called 'the election team'; a task force, dedicated to that. They had been preparing for 'D-day', as we called it, for a month. They worked hard. They were in the polling stations and made sure everything went right. We had someone in each station. It was so well done the other parties were very surprised. They weren't represented in every station. We were represented everywhere, which was very important—our members were ready to go anywhere."

They set up a new online platform, so that people who couldn't vote online were able to connect with other people who could vote for them. "The other parties usually just leave it to people to organise themselves among the family. We set up a platform specifically for people who couldn't vote, making sure that their vote would not get lost." (In France, it is possible to vote by proxy, and about 4% of citizens do.)

Stefan Egger spent the election day of 2013 in the NEOSphere, the NEOS HQ in Vienna: "It was incredibly hard" he remembered. "It felt like the whole campaign over again. It seemed endless. In the afternoon, conflicting reports came in—from certainly out, to a surprise success. Over time, that solidified to certainly in—not astonishing, but definitely exhilarating. And then came the exit poll's bar chart."

Learning from Failure

Failure at the voting booth is always a possibility for a start-up. Momentum had that experience on April 8, 2018. The Hungarian National Assembly is a unicameral body consisting of 199 members elected for four-year terms. The electoral threshold to enter is 5%. In a mix between a ballot and a proportional system, voters choose MPs from 106 single-member districts in one ballot, while 93 party-list seats are allocated according to a combination of a second ballot and "wasted votes" from the first ballot.

On election day, the polling stations for the Hungarian national election are supposed to close at 7 pm. At the time, however, the Hungarian TV station M1 still showed long queues in front of the polling stations. To allow more people to vote, the polls were kept open for longer. It was already clear that there would be an exceptionally high voter turnout.

In Budapest, opposition activists staged a party in front of the Parliament, under heavy police guard. Meanwhile, at the Momentum election party, the mood was cautiously optimistic. Everything was illuminated in violet, the party colour. About 300 people, most in their mid-20s, were chatting, upbeat but nervous. Shortly before 9 pm, however, the positive mood shifted to anger. The Head of the Electoral Board said 2500 voters were still waiting to cast their votes. They had been queuing for hours.

The election observers of the OSCE (Organization for Security and Co-operation in Europe) announced a press conference for the following day after numerous reports of irregularities by Orban's governing Fidesz party. Among them was an audio recording obtained by Hungary's largest private TV station that seemed to indicate votes had been bought. FIDESZ voters were also alleged to have been transported to Pécs, a city in the Southwest, to vote there. There was also talk of polling stations closing down, despite long queues of people waiting to vote.

Around 10 pm, alleged "preliminary results" were leaked to the press that pointed to a FIDESZ majority, despite the fact that the Electoral Board had announced there would be no results before 11.30 pm. There were still queues in front of the polling station in Budapest XI, where people who didn't live in Budapest could vote.

Shortly before 11 pm, the first results were announced. They indicated that FIDESZ would regain its two-thirds supermajority in the National Assembly. Momentum was projected to be 2.64%, which was not enough to enter Parliament. In the end, after taking into account postal ballots, this figure would grow to 3.1%, but at the time, there was a strong sense of disappointment among the Momentum people. And also anxiety: what would become of Hungary now Orban had regained a supermajority?

The atmosphere lightened when Momentum Chairman and frontrunner, András Fekete-Győr, gave a stump speech. The result might not have led Momentum into Parliament, but it was enough to assure considerable public funding for the party from then on. Activists were brought to the stage, people hugged. "If you had told me a year ago that Momentum would reach more than 3%, and 175,000 voters in the elections" András told me a few weeks later on Skype, "I would not have believed you." It was a strong showing. Could it have been even stronger?

There were seven important areas where Momentum could have done better, even in such a highly challenging environment as Viktor Orban's Hungary. They provide useful lessons for other political start-ups:

- Transforming the party into a campaign machine
- Programme development versus fieldwork
- Internal alignment
- Positioning
- Messages
- Fundraising
- Building awareness
- Credibility

Transforming the party into a campaign machine "A campaign is a machine. Momentum wasn't a machine," Katka Cseh told me via Skype in April 2018, a couple of weeks after the election. She had just taken a couple of days off, and was "more chilled than usual." Looking back with a little distance, she said "we had to go from a group of friends, who were very close to each other, to a very professional organisation."

As with any start-up, initial homogeneity of the founding group is a success factor for political enterprises. But when the enterprise begins to grow rapidly, it must be able to accommodate increasing diversity. To do that, it has to become more professional. Momentum did not manage that transformation well. "And the party is still struggling with this kind of professionalisation" Cseh admitted. "We made that mistake for a long time. The local chapters still functioned as groups of friends, instead of as parts of a political party. It was hard to make changes."

Programme development versus fieldwork "Another mistake we made was to try meet each and every expectation of the people" said András Fekete-Győr. "So we worked out the most thorough political programme. I would not say no one cared about it, but very few people voted for Momentum because of its programme." Of course a political start-up needs a programme, as does any movement that seeks to enter Parliament. The impression I got from several of my interviews, however, was that liberal and centrist start-ups in particular are prone to become overly ambitious in developing their programmes to the last detail. That ties up scarce resources that are desperately needed elsewhere, especially for fieldwork. That was an area where Momentum was not so successful, as Fekete-Győr conceded: "We did not really have experienced local candidates. The Momentum membership consisted mainly of people who hadn't been engaged with politics before. We therefore did not know well how to establish ourselves and grow in the local communities. This is an area where Momentum failed, and where we need to be much more organised, professional and aggressive in the future."

Internal alignment Keeping the band together while moving at high velocity is a major challenge for political start-ups. Constant internal communication is the key here. "I think this was the biggest challenge for Momentum", Fekete-Győr told me during our Skype interview, "transparency. The Presidency, the Board and the Directors were remote from the average Momentum member. If I had the chance over again, I would put much more focus on this, and communicate more with the Momentum members, for example through live videos, or Q&A forums. We did this of course, but people still want more information. This is where I want to be more active. I think for every party on earth, that is an on-going challenge."

When emotions run high and things start to escalate, avoiding conflicts altogether or effectively managing them, is crucial to campaign success. As the "group of friends" it was, Momentum seemed to have a hard time doing that. "There was a lot of infighting in December and January" recalled Csaba Tóth, a Hungarian political scientist I talked to via Skype a month after the election in May 2018, "so they lost two months, when they concentrated on internal issues." Cseh agreed: "It harmed the party. And as it was in the press, it was also harmful externally." Internal communications were leaked to the press. "There were stories like 'Momentum is falling apart', at a very crucial time" says Cseh.

It began as a disagreement between the Campaign and Communications managers. "We wanted to remove the Head of Communications, because we weren't satisfied with how things were working" said Cseh. "But because he was one of the oldest members, his friends were extremely upset." The situation quickly escalated into a huge conflict. "And then, ironically, both the Campaign and the Communications managers left the party." Momentum had to change key personnel at a late stage in the campaign. "It was about trivial things, minor internal dynamics. It blew up, and they spent two months arguing." It was two months the party could not make up for when the campaign really needed to take off.

Positioning The Hungarian opposition is a crowded and fragmented field. Momentum had a lot of competition. "Especially from the Green party, also known as the 'Politics can be different'-party" said Toth. "The Greens had a lot of money, and targeted a similar electorate—younger, more mobile, more European." Founded as recently as 2009, the Greens also exemplified a new kind of party. They had already entered Parliament in 2010, and re-entered in 2014. In the end, they got 7.1%, four percentage points more than Momentum.

How could Momentum have positioned themselves better in such a situation? By highlighting one of their key differences, Toth now believes: either in ideology and political outlook—Momentum is clearly a more liberal party, even if the label is not as positive in Hungarian politics as elsewhere—or by transmitting an anti-system message. The Greens, after all, had been in the Parliament for eight years. They were as much a part of the system Momentum was challenging as the other parties.

Messages Momentum's unclear positioning had consequences for its campaign messages. "They made a mistake" Toth explained. "It was clear that although their party represented generational change, and a new type of politics, they couldn't win through young people alone. The math just doesn't add up. If you ignore everyone above 40, you would need 25% of those below 40 to get to 5%, due to turnout and demographics." Momentum was a small urban party with an educated base. They could afford not to focus on villages, but they could not afford to ignore middle aged and especially older people, because they accounted for too large a proportion of the electorate.

Toth thinks that, in the end, the generational-change message, which resonates even with older people, evolved during the campaign. It went from "you know, 'these people have had their chance, so let's have new people' to 'we are a new generation'; from 'we need young people' to 'we're the party of the youth', which does not necessarily appeal to older voters. So I think they became too generational."

Toth said he could imagine an election where this would work. But the Hungarian election in 2018 had a very high turnout, especially among older people. At the same time, there was no increase in the youth turn-out. As he said, the numbers just didn't add up in the end.

Fundraising Ironically, Momentum had too much money too late in the campaign, thanks to the rules of Hungarian state funding.

Once Momentum had submitted their 106 candidates for all the districts at the beginning of March, each of whom had collected 500 signatures, they got €1.2 million. All of it had to be spent in the three weeks from Mid-March to April 8. It might already have been too late at that point. The reason for this was that they had too little money in the critical earlier stages of the campaign. "Not because they didn't try—they did raise some money, but of course it's Hungary, which makes it more difficult" said Momentum's Cseh. "We did some fundraising, but it wasn't very successful."

Building awareness In Hungary, media and free media only penetrate parts of the population. "Half of the population you cannot really reach via the Internet" Tóth explained, "you can only really reach them through outdoor media, through local rallies or through one of the big TV channels. That is a structural factor of how you reach your voters. Obviously, the main voter base was reached by Momentum, but they could have picked up some more votes. Momentum was not really well known in a large part of the population."

Momentum mainly advertised through social media. They needed money to get their big-scale advertising started, but they did not have enough. Once state funding poured in, "from March 15, they were everywhere." And it worked: according to polls, 7% of late deciders went for Momentum. In stark contrast, only 2% of the early deciders did so. "If that 1 or 2% in the villages had heard from them, they would have voted for them" Toth believes. "If they had had one more month for the campaign, they could have been successful."

Credibility Credibility as a young cosmopolitan alternative to Orban was one of Momentum's strengths. But, image-wise, it was also one of their weaknesses.

"It's OK to have lots of young people in a party, OK to have the young generation" said Toth. "But the other parties that were successful had people in their leadership who had professional track records, and were, at least in some areas of their lives, successful—academics, entrepreneurs, people who had actually done something. Momentum was led by people who had never really done anything. They were all under 30, so the party had this youth movement feeling. For the next election, they need to have people who have expertise or competence, or at least the image of it. That, of course, is difficult because it compromises the generational-change message. If you want purity, you cannot have anyone above 30." But for a political start-up, credibility is more important than purity.

The future of Momentum

Where does Momentum go from here? Katka Cseh is quite optimistic for their role as extra-parliamentary opposition: "Parliament is seen as really dysfunctional. Related to that, we have a lot of people applying to work with us, literally thousands. For many, we are perceived as the last alternative."

Momentum were around 1500 people before the election. In the weeks following the election, 5000 people applied to join Momentum. "An incredible amount" András Fekete-Győr states proudly. "All the parties that have managed to enter Parliament have lost some of their charm. In the eyes of the people, they became part of the system, operating under a two thirds-Fidesz majority. We can now be a credible movement."

To manage the "on-boarding" of those several thousand new members, they have around 100 local "buddies" in every large Hungarian city. Every newcomer is connected with a buddy, who is then responsible for integrating him or her. They also have a 60-strong volunteer-operated "Momentum HR team", who support the local buddies. "We had a very big camp with 300 people a few weeks ago. Every two weeks we want to stage an event where our politicians are talking to the new members, where we barbecue. . ." Fekete-Győr told me. He has ambitious plans for the future: "I would like for our local buddies to establish local 'problem plans'— what are the local problems, how do the locals feel about politics, what can Momentum do for them? And then we can work on the answers."

Fekete-Győr is particularly optimistic for the European elections in 2019. "Because, as the generation that has been abroad a lot, thanks to the Erasmus-programme of the European Union, we have a lot of experience in Europe, and we are the only political party in Hungary which has a Europe-wide network. In Germany alone we have five Momentum organisations. In Vienna, we have a very strong Momentum organisation. That will make us appealing to the voters who are passionate about Europe."

In 2017, on May 1, the date when Hungary joined the EU, they held a large demonstration under the banner 'We Belong to Europe'. More than 10,000 people attended. "When Vladimir Putin visited Viktor Orban last August, we organised a protest march. In the eyes of the Hungarian people, we are affiliating with the European project, and that will help us."

Toth agrees: "I think they have a lot of potential. They have a very good chance of making it to the European Parliament." The election will take place a little more than a year after the Hungarian election, in May 2019. Momentum is Hungary's most pro-European party. That should give it a unique market position. The main threat is a resumption of the infighting, Toth warned. "You know, finger pointing. It's a tendency they have. They also have a tendency to make internal processes too bureaucratic. That was one of the reasons for the infighting. A lot of power lies with the members, who have less stake in the election results than the candidates."

Momentum will, therefore, be "working on some internal reforms, to professionalise the party" said Cseh. "We hired some professionals for that. So hopefully we will have a more prepared organisation ahead of the next election."

Ciudadanos: Defeat and Triumph

Ciudadanos also swallowed the bitter pill of failure in Spain in 2008. Three years after their founding on the regional level, and two years after their successful entry into the Catalan regional parliament with 3.0%, Ciudadanos bombed at the national level. "We went into that election. Complete disaster. No representation whatsoever" recalled Jose Manuel Villegas. They received 46,313 votes, or 0.2%, in the Spanish general election. The overwhelming winner was the Spanish Socialist Party of Jose Luis Zapatero, with 42.6%.

Ciudadanos's ambition was to grow beyond Catalonia, and become competitive nationally. In 2008, it was too early for them. That experience left the party in such shock that having returned to the Catalan Parliament with three representatives in 2010, they did not run at all in the general election the following year. This time, the conservative Partido Popular of Mariano Rajoy won with 40.1%.

The party competed again in the Catalan regional election in 2012. This time they gained 7.6% and nine seats, six more than in 2010. Based on this success, they started plotting a strategy for the national level. This time would be different. There was enough time until the next expected election, and no need to rush. They would build something sustainable, step by step. "Instead of going nationally again just for the sake of it, the idea was to follow the same strategy that we had done in Catalonia; to create a kind of civic movement" Villegas explained. "We started touring Spain, organising events and trying to find out if there was really room for Ciudadanos to go into national politics."

As in Catalonia in 2006, they published a manifesto you could subscribe to, this time online, without becoming a party member. But you had to leave your contact data. Some 70,000 people subscribed.

That was the first sign that this time would be different. It was. The first confirmation they had got things right this time came in 2014, with the European elections. Ciudadanos gained 3.16%, and two seats in the European Parliament. The following year, at the Spanish General elections, Ciudadanos came the second, after Left-wing populists, Podemos, scooping a sensational 40 seats, or 13.9% of the vote.

Election campaigns pose unreasonable demands on people's lives. They are undemocratic, and often unsuccessful, particularly for political start-ups. So why do people give up their jobs to participate in them?

"Until the end, I had the feeling that this was something I must be part of. It all felt right," Stefan Egger of NEOS explained. "At times, it was incredibly hard. At times it was devastatingly unprofessional. Had anybody watched, he or she might have concluded this couldn't work. But there was so much positive energy." The political context at the time, and the sense that there was a window where things might happen gave them lots of optimism, and further strengthened their spirits.

"I am a compulsive optimist by nature. I always see things positively: 'alles wird gut' (everything is going to be fine)", Egger explained to me. "That approach bound me strongly to NEOS. And then I have phases where I turn from realistic to almost pessimistic; when I look at the facts. You won't join such a campaign if you focus only on the facts. You will never have the budget you planned; never enough activists; and never the structures that would be sensible at the time. If you think like that, you have already lost. On the other hand, if you only have people who live on hope, you will also lose. It takes a mix of people who create the necessary structure, and who at the same time thrive on an optimism that provides them with energy and belief."

Success in politics requires the head and the heart.

We entered Parliament, and everything was over.

Feri Thierry (in conversation)

On 29 September 2013, NEOS entered Parliament. We partied hard through the night in a light-headed, anything-goes frame of mind. Some, including myself, talked about NEOS now having a shot at coalition talks. Of course, that was mere wishful thinking. The reality was, even if the "Grand Coalition" of Social Democrats and Conservatives had been badly defeated, it had not been finished. Somehow, between the two of them, they had managed to just stay above the 50% required to prolong their unholy marriage.

The mood changed the day after the election. The new reality was kicking in. So many decisions now had to be taken within a couple of weeks. The NEOS Board retreated into day-long consultations, while staff were standing outside, not knowing whether they would have an employment contract the next day. There simply had been no plan for the scenario of getting in. But even if there had been a plan, the emotional exhaustion left most reeling. Wear and tear often only show up in the aftermath. Now that the 24/7 stress was over, many suffered from a "relief depression". A kind of political baby blues. It had been a wild, and sometimes overwhelming, ride.

Also, the prospects were uncertain. NEOS was in Parliament. It had been thrust onto the public stage. There was no flying under the radar anymore. In addition to the party organisation, a parliamentary group had to be built, and quickly. If the public did not watch, political opponents certainly would.

Facing up to the tasks right in front of us was made even harder by the hype that set in immediately after the successful election. In the media, NEOS was portrayed as a successful, young and hip party, which seemed to operate in a different century than the traditional ones. In the polls, NEOS started climbing, and continued to do so for a period of 4 months. The initial depression was soon superimposed by a

© Springer Nature Switzerland AG 2019
J. Lentsch, *Political Entrepreneurship*,
https://doi.org/10.1007/978-3-030-02861-9_9

collective mania—a kind of organisation bi-polar disorder set in. What felt like a relief at first really was a very unstable and untethered emotional mess to operate in.

In Poland, Nowoczesna's first task, after the successful election, was to find out who was in Parliament, and who wasn't. "There were a couple of surprises" Miłosz Hodun told me. "We wouldn't have expected to win a mandate in those two constituencies." They won 29 seats in the Sejm (the lower house), and arranged meetings with their new parliamentarians. They had screened them all, of course, but because of the time-compressed campaign, with only 6 months from founding to election, they simply did not know all of them very well. Most were new to politics. They had to learn everything from scratch—how Parliament works, which committees to focus on. The central question was "Yes, we are in, but what next? What do we do now?"

En Marche was also in for a rough awakening. "We won", Aziz François Ndiaye said of the day after the election of Emmanuel Macron as President of France, "and then we started to get scared." You go from zero to hero. And then you realise you actually can go *back* again, from hero to zero. The day before, you had nothing to lose. Now you have everything to lose.

More than that: you had to continue winning. En Marche had little more than *1 month* between the election of the President and the national assembly election. Without a majority in the Assemblée Nationale "we knew we couldn't implement the programme" Ndiaye explained. Macron's acceptance speech and his appearance at the Louvre, where the Anthem of Europe was played, were emotional highlights, but knowing what was to come, En Marche staff did not really enjoy the celebrations.

Entering parliament means you suddenly have to manage the problem of success. It is a good problem to have but "the hardest part for most organisations is knowing what to do when they succeed" (Ries, 2017). This applies to political as much as to business start-ups.

In a blog written 4 months after the electoral success, NEOS-Managing Director Feri Thierry described Day 1 and the subsequent weeks as follows:

"We suddenly faced a plethora of questions and challenges: the employment contracts all expired the day after the election, the lease agreement was terminable, the budget had been planned up to election day, but there was no plan whatsoever for the time after that."

There is no defined working process for establishing a new party, no fixed allocation of tasks, no well-rehearsed sequences. "This leads to the situation where ordering a newspaper subscription takes about 30 different decisions and other activities. You have to be clear about the legal basics for political parties, that decisions are made by people or bodies competent to make them, that there is a clear allocation of responsibilities, and much more. In a few months I will smile at all of this, but at the moment we are facing a huge mountain of work" ("Aus dem Leben eines Parteigeschäftsführers", NEOS, February 19, 2014).

"You realise that what you do is completely inefficient, but right now, you can't do it any other way" Thierry would tell me later.

And the mountain grew by the hour. Now that NEOS was in, numerous national and international journalists wanted to have interviews. There was a parliamentary group to set up. For this, NEOS had quickly to recruit people for the various staff positions. Literally hundreds of unsolicited applications landed in the inbox within the first few days. Within weeks, we were facing cognitive as well as operational overload.

Everyone had focused on winning. Nobody had prepared for having won.

As Thierry recalled: "You have to drive a car on the highway at 180 km per hour, while you are busy building it. That was the exact feeling I had."

In retrospect, although not at the time, it's clear that there were some key tasks that had to be addressed after entering parliament.

9.1   Re-integrating

"Within just a few weeks, in an incredible intensity, we built up the whole organisation" said Thierry, when I asked him about his post-electoral period as the Executive Director of NEOS. But a political enterprise that enters parliament has to build more than one organisation. In the case of NEOS, the three "entities", as they were called, that had to be built right away were the party, the parliamentary group, and the academy, which I helped set up and subsequently led. Building those three from scratch offered the opportunity to avoid some of the mistakes and antiquated structures of traditional parties. But it also made apparent the essential need to align them, and keep them aligned. After all, each of the three organisations operated according in its own logic The party was tasked with winning elections, the group was tasked with winning arguments in the political arena, and the academy was tasked with longer-term development of people and policies. (see "Design for unity in diversity", Sect. 6.4).

Accordingly, starting with the first election, NEOS has adopted the practice after an election of running a structured post-election process via an extensive series of retreats at various levels. The objective of these retreats, facilitated by external consultants who are often organisational development specialists, is to help re-integrate the growing or at least changing organisation that is NEOS, at a higher level of complexity.

In the case of the 2013 election, however, the need to re-integrate was even more complex. NEOS had run on an electoral platform together with the Liberal Forum and Julis. With few historical exceptions (notably, CDU/CSU in Germany), such platforms tend to break up following success. The joint project has been achieved, and the partners are not dependent on each other anymore. Consequently, the centrifugal forces become overpowering.

The Boards of NEOS and the Liberal Forum therefore decided to merge under the name of "NEOS—The New Austria and Liberal Forum". The merger was completed in January, 2014. It was an emotional moment for us all. After the merger, Julis (Young Liberals) were renamed Junos (Young Liberal NEOS), and became the official youth organisation of NEOS. As would happen repeatedly, NEOS had managed to re-integrate itself on a higher level of organisational complexity.

9.2   Re-engaging

Staff, candidates and volunteers had all worked tirelessly towards one day—the day of the election. Once it was over, and success had been celebrated, the journey of some, including a candidate who had become an MP and a staff member who had become a parliamentary assistant, continued in prescribed ways. But it is important to realise that such people are only a small minority. For the overwhelming majority of the comrades-in-arms, most of all the volunteers, the journey had no clearly defined continuation. That may lead to confusion, frustration and even depression. The objective had been achieved—now what? For the leadership of a political start-up, this is quite a challenge. There are so many things to do, such as building up the parliamentary group, that taking care of and offering volunteers opportunities to re-engage quickly and meaningfully, may be pushed down on the list of priorities. That is a mistake that could come back to haunt the political start-up.

Beate Meinl-Reisinger, who would later become Chairwoman and Group Leader of NEOS, remembered a meaningful encounter when she was contesting the Viennese elections for NEOS:

"As top-candidate for Vienna, I was making the rounds, introducing myself. One of the people I met was Jessi Lintl, then a Member of Parliament for Team Stronach [the populist political start-up of Austrian billionaire Frank Stronach, see page 120]. I asked her what they did with all the active people from the campaign; 'how do you continue engaging them?' And she said, 'Well, nothing really; when there is another campaign, they will be back'. My only thought was 'bullshit. You have to be proactive about engaging people to retain them'." Team Stronach did not survive its first term in Parliament.

On a larger scale Barack Obama's campaign team faced this problem in 2008, after he became President of the United States. They had managed to build a huge, volunteer-driven movement, with a technology-supported organisation, that had no precedent in political history. They tried to keep it alive, but it slowly fizzled out after Obama took office. The movement had successfully completed its project, but it had no answer to the volunteers, when they asked "what next?". But movements need projects to keep them going and growing.

En Marche includes key people and advisors who experienced the Obama campaigns of 2008 and 2012 first hand. As Guillaume Liegey observed: "It is interesting what they want to do with the movement now: all the efforts of Obama with Organising for America, to try to sustain the movement after his elections in 2008 and 2012, failed. En Marche is trying to find a way to make it work. They're putting a lot of resources into that."

One thing they're considering is using technology-assisted "listening campaigns" as a standard tool. As with La Grande Marche, but on a smaller scale, they try to compile qualitative citizen feedback to create a real-time evidence-based image of a certain department or city. For this, they plan to train activists as "civic pollsters".

Other parties have already started to adopt a similar approach. It will be interesting to see what comes of this.

9.3 Consolidating

Election campaigns cost a lot of money. The political start-up will have often taken out large bank loans to cover its costs. These need to be paid back. If the costs have exceeded the budget, the election result was below expectations or mistakes have messed up the financial planning, some tough conversations will follow and some tough decisions will have to be made. "Nobody wants to pay your fixed costs" Nowoczesna founder, Ryszard Petru, told me, "and nobody is happy to pay your debts." After the mistake of Nowoczesna's treasurer (see page 156), which cost them the entire party subsidy for the whole period, Nowoczesna was suddenly facing an unexpected financial challenge. "This is a very unattractive proposition for both the potential donor and the receiving party: 'Would you be so kind to pay my debts?'"

Some loans can be extended, others may be forgiven, but still the start-up may not have the resources it expected to have. It may have to prune the existing structure, in order to survive. At the same time, the start-up needs the resources to build up capacity—otherwise, it may starve to death financially. In any case, post-election is the time for tough financial decisions, because the next election is never far away.

9.4 Offboarding People (The Right Way)

Post-election is also the time for tough personnel decisions. Trying to keep everyone on board is the right thing to do, in principle. But there may be situations when 'clear and severe', is better than trying to mend something that is broken for good, and may deteriorate further. Right after entering Parliament is a good time to focus energy internally. It marks the final transition of the party from a feel-good start-up to a professional organisation. It is therefore a good time to try to resolve conflicts you may have avoided or kept a lid on during the campaign, or to make a dispassionate decision about whether a particular conflict is resolvable.

Some of those conflicts may be more complex than others (for example, if they involve newly-elected MPs), but they all tie up energy internally that will very soon have to be focused externally. Post-election is, therefore, a bad time to drag out those conflicts. The conversations may be hard, but the consequences of avoiding them may be even harder later. After all, every staff member, volunteer and representative is a voter, and has voters associated with him or her. And, as they say, you always meet twice in life.

Therefore, if the conclusion is to part ways, it will also be wise to try to do so on the best possible terms. After successful elections, if the situation allows, generosity should be shown particularly to those whose journeys are at an end. After all, they made their personal contribution in time, energy end maybe even money, for the benefit of others. For staff, that may mean helping them find new jobs, at the very least. For volunteers, that may mean providing them with face-to-face time with the leadership team.

In politics, however, you cannot simply let go of some people, even if the case for that is crystal-clear. You need to accept that, and find a way to work with them. That may be the best possible outcome of such a conversation.

Whatever the constraints, the leadership team has to make sure that the right people are in the right places at the start of the parliamentary term, on all levels. Beginnings matter in politics, for election periods, as well as for political parties.

9.5   Re-focusing

Getting acquainted with parliamentary procedures can tie up all the energy, not only of the parliamentary group, but also of the political start-up as a whole. While a solid parliamentary performance is certainly important, it is even more important to re-focus as much energy as possible externally.

Nowoczesna did that very well in 2016, under very tough circumstances.

Despite the mistake of their treasurer (see next page), which meant that the party lost out on all public funding for the whole period, they had an excellent first year. "For us it was success after success" Miłosz Hodun told me, during my visit to the Nowoczesna headquarters in Warsaw in February, 2017. "We showed the electorate that Civic Platform were no longer the leaders of the opposition. Even though they had over 115 MPs, and we only had 30, journalists and citizens saw us as leaders of the opposition. Our MPs, especially the women, were on TV all the time. In the parliament, they took part in every discussion. And when the crisis with the constitutional court started, and Civic Platform protested and walked out, it was our 30 MPs against 240 from PiS. We debated with them the whole night. And people watched it live, because it was only the beginning of the crisis. People couldn't believe what they were seeing. So that was the first moment when we showed people that we, not the people who left the room, were the real opposition leaders."

PiS did not give Nowoczesna time to go on holidays, but this baptism of political fire and the fact that Nowoczesna withstood the pressure, gave them a strong boost in the polls, pushing them above 20%. One MP in particular, Kamila Gasiuk-Pihowicz, stood out. She was in her early 1930s and an unknown. "She became a star" said Hodun. "She was a very emotional, really good speaker." In 2018, Gasiuk-Pihowicz became leader of Nowoczesna's parliamentary group.

9.6   Rookie Mistakes

Getting into parliament causes acute mental overload. What you have not thought through or planned beforehand, you certainly cannot think through now. When you are overloaded, you make mistakes. Balls get dropped, opportunities are missed. As noted above, NEOS received hundreds of applications in the first couple of weeks after entering parliament, some of them no one responded to. What a tragedy—they were all people who wanted to work with us!

Looking back to the time around elections, administrative mistakes were among the most common identified by the political entrepreneurs I interviewed. Basic contingency planning might have prevented some of them.

But, as Nowoczesna learned the hard way, no contingency plan in the world can prevent some mistakes. For their campaign, they took out a bank loan of €500,000, and transferred the sum to the wrong bank account. Instead of the account of the election committee, the money went into the party's account. The difference between the accounts was only 4 digits, and one click. The treasurer typed in the wrong numbers, and couldn't undo it. The PiS Government rejoiced, and denied Nowoczesna funding for the whole period. In consequence, on entering, Nowoczesna lost a party subsidy of €2 million per year. They appealed to the Supreme Court, but to no avail. The law is the law.

In Austria, right after the successful 2013 election, our amazement with ourselves was accentuated by a sudden upswing of support for the new parliamentary party. "Nothing succeeds like success", as they say. Suddenly everyone seemed always to have known that NEOS would make it. All the experts who before the election had explained why a NEOS success was impossible, now went live explaining why it had been inevitable. Everyone, it seemed, had voted for the party, when in fact only 5% had done so. NEOS was sexy. Hype set in. Within weeks, the party shot up in the opinion polls. At the beginning of 2014, NEOS climbed to 15%, even surpassing the Greens for the first time.

Imagine what it must be like seeing your start-up shares skyrocket after successfully going public on the stock exchange. It would be hard to resist the hype.

We believed the hype. We were riding the wave that we thought to be of our own making. It is hard to stay self-critical when everyone you meet says you are great. Like the Roman generals during their triumphal processions, we should have had somebody whisper in our ears "Memento mori!"—remember that you will die. We felt we could do no wrong, while we were, in fact, making tons of mistakes. Our overconfidence was our weakness, and our blind spot. The political competition just had to wait for the inevitable mistakes.

In addition to administrative mistakes, we made communication mistakes. Some of those were unforced errors; others were provoked by much more experienced opponents. On one occasion, we fell into the trap of not distancing ourselves enough from the idea of privatising water (which was never our policy). It provoked a media outcry, and alienated our base. The idea was and still is anathema to Austrians. On another occasion, we adopted the policy of calling for the legalisation of Cannabis almost by accident, and then publicised the decision in a very ambivalent way. The first instance allowed the competition to paint us as cold and neoliberal. The second instance allowed them to portray us as flippant and amateurish. Both characterisations undermined voters' trust in us as a serious contender for a party in government. The labels have stuck. October, 2014 was the last time we polled in double figures.

Growing Up and Handing Over

10

> *In 2014, when the party really started at a Spanish level, it was me and an intern. That was it. And that was the reason I had to drive everywhere myself.*
>
> Fran Hervías

Stéphane Roques had "never, never been involved with politics". He had quite a career though, at the intersections of the private, public and third sectors. "It was not usual business. Never with me." To begin with he worked for 6 years with a "Big Five" consultancy, where he was in charge of auditing and consulting for non-profits, such as associations, foundations, social interest businesses, as well as public sector institutions. One of his clients was of particular interest to him: Médecins Sans Frontières (Doctors Without Borders), which he joined during a year-long sabbatical to participate in their disaster and humanitarian relief work on the ground.

He left the consultancy to become the General Director of Groupe AFM-Téléthon, an association composed of patients (and their families) suffering from neuromuscular disease, and rare genetic illnesses. So at the age of 33, Roques was managing one of France's largest fundraising events, and four entities with 600 staff and €100 million of turnover, focused on research into those diseases and the development of innovative therapies.

At Groupe AFM he learned valuable lessons about how to work with people with "very different agendas and goals", and various stakeholders: "the public, patients, pharma [the pharmaceutical industry] and others. I was dealing with business, doctors, the public sector—but on behalf of patients, for patients, reporting to patients." This taught him how to be in charge of "militants" (highly committed volunteers and activists). He learned to use the strength of a lot of people and their social commitment in dealing with the authorities.

© Springer Nature Switzerland AG 2019
J. Lentsch, *Political Entrepreneurship*,
https://doi.org/10.1007/978-3-030-02861-9_10

Following an internal crisis at Médecins Sans Frontières, he became their CEO, managing 6000 staff in the US, Japan, Australia and France, with missions in 40 countries. His job was to re-organise MSF, and push through a new internal policy to delegate responsibility, autonomy and power to the field. This was also something that would be of importance later.

In 2016, after more than 3 years leading MSF, he read Emmanuel Macron's book "Révolution: C'est notre combat pour la France" (Revolution: This is our fight for France, op. cit.). Suddenly, he told me, "everything was crystal-clear. As a way to deal with social issues it was exactly what I wanted. How to deal with problems, to be solution-oriented, to be more dedicated to impact and solutions than to internal games." He was also impressed by Macron's intellect, and his approach of "en même temps" (at the same time), which meant you do not necessarily have to trade things off against each other: you can protect the environment and help the economy grow, at the same time. "To me" Roques told me, "this was absolutely clever and smart. In my career, I have always been doing both, like being at the consultancy and at MSF at the same time."

After the end of his mandate as CEO of MSF, he joined En Marche in November 2016, 6 months before the Presidential election. He was very involved in his local political committee, and decided to run in the primaries. When he was not selected because of the algorithm that gender-balanced the list of En Marche-candidates, the woman who was selected asked him to be her deputy. He agreed. "I wanted to help Macron, so to be number one or two didn't matter. We ran a strong local campaign, and won."

He then became a "helper" at the En Marche headquarter in Paris, responding to voters' emails and other things. "Obviously I was the oldest helper. I'm still one of the oldest here, at 45."

In July 2017, En Marche started to look for a new General Director. He applied and was appointed.

Think big. Start small. *Scale fast.* This is way of the political enterprise. At the same time, scaling fast poses huge challenges. And, as Johanna Mair and Christian Seelos argue in their book ("Innovation and Scaling for Impact: How Effective Social Enterprises Do it", Stanford University Press, 2017), and as Ciudadanos found out in 2008, scaling *too* fast can be a strategic mistake. Even when scaling is the right thing to do, when complexity grows, the organisation needs to continuously be re-integrated in all its dimensions—strategy, structure, culture and execution.

In other words, organisation needs to be scaled in line with growth. Organisational development needs to become the focus, and may trigger projects accordingly. It may also mean an upgrade, quantitatively as much as qualitatively, in personnel. That does not mean the previous staff were no good—quite the contrary, they helped to bring about the success. But consolidating and creating a much larger organisation needs additional and more diverse skills. Also, skills and experience that were previously out of reach financially can, and should, now be afforded. This can be a bitter pill to swallow for staff who have worked really hard and, having achieved success, now expect to be rewarded with more responsibility, and promoted to higher offices. Although this is perfectly understandable, it makes for tough choices for the leadership. Making the wrong call on campaign staff and volunteers who put their trust in their leaders may lead to deep to disappointments, and the loss of valuable talent and experience. But making the wrong call in their favour may limit growth potential, or worse, a failure to consolidate on the respective stage of organisational development.

No political enterprise, to date, has scaled faster than En Marche. It won the presidency and a parliamentary majority with barely a year of its foundation as a movement. Its challenges are a magnifying glass for other political start-ups that started at the national level, and quickly focused down to the regional level.

10.1 Top-Down

According to Stéphane Roques, En Marche now faces three main challenges, and three main goals.

Firstly, as a political movement, En Marche will need to work with the Executive, the Prime Minister, and parliament. It will need to be one of the five political actors—the President, the Élysée, ministers, parliament, and the movement—that will have to act together, if Macron's transformative plans are to succeed.

"It's a strong challenge" Roques admits, "because everything is new. We have to have the same DNA, the same spirit. So it helps to be connected. But we need to work at that. We have to mobilise the field, to consult the public. But we don't have to be 100% aligned; we are not the government."

Secondly, En Marche needs to organise and mobilise nationwide, and improve its political organisation, together with its members, representatives, and activists. This is where Obama failed. He had his movement behind him up to the election, but then it broke down, and fizzled out. This is where En Marche wants to do better. That it won't easy has already become apparent with the conflicts around their first post-electoral General Assembly, where activists cast doubt on Macron's ability to push through his reform agenda, and challenged the party structure as undemocratic.

"We need to resume working on the movement" said Roques. "But we need to make sure we keep our DNA. If you don't manage the freedom members have, it's not productive. The challenge is how to be efficient and democratic at the same time. It's one of the current challenges. For me, it's a real intellectual debate; 100 departments, 3.3 million French people abroad. . .".

Thirdly, En Marche faces the challenge of developing new ideas. It needs to keep identifying new ways to do politics differently, and despite being in government, to stay constantly self-critical, so that we remain open and capable of integrating the thoughts of other people who may not be En Marche or French.

"We need to be able to push new ideas, new concepts, to continue to re-generate ourselves" Roques continued. "One of the reasons for the failure of the traditional parties was clearly becoming disconnected from the field, totally disconnected from the French people. There was a huge gap. They also failed to re-generate themselves regularly. Society is moving too fast today. If you want to be able to listen to society, understand it, and propose a societal project, you need to be connected, you need to be in the field, not only in the big Palais in Paris."

That this is easier said than done, Roques had to acknowledge himself—after 11 months as Director General of En Marche, in July 2018 he moved on to become CEO of the biocluster Medicen Paris Region's, to foster collaborative projects in the healthcare sector, and attract more innovative start-ups to the region.

10.2 Bottom-Up

Fran Hervías, now Ciudadanos' Secretary of Organisation, and the right-hand of Jose Manuel Villegas, the General Secretary, is a warm and amusing person. Before joining Ciudadanos, he had a professional career as a meteorologist, and was working for the meteorological services in Catalonia, "a safe job". It was what he had studied and what he had always wanted.

But he saw how bad things were in Catalonia with corruption and rising nationalism, and wanted to do something about it. "And then in 2010, I had to choose between coming into politics fulltime as a job, and leaving my personal career, or staying on my career path. I saw the situation in Catalonia was bad enough, so I thought I needed to prioritise my involvement and sacrifice my professional career, to help the party."

As the Secretary of Organisation, he is responsible for looking after 13,000 registered members, building up the party's regional structure, co-ordinating electoral campaigns ("Seven in the last two and a half years. It has been crazy."), and expanding Ciudadanos in the rest of Spain.

Of all the political start-ups portrayed in this book Ciudadanos is the only one that scaled bottom-up. They were founded on the regional level and first entered the regional parliament of Catalonia. They established the national organisation, and entered the Spanish parliament almost a decade later.

After their defeat in the 2007 Spanish general election, they started to prepare for their second attempt following their success at the 2012 Catalan regional elections, where they more than doubled their percentage from 3.4 to 7.6%. At the end of this process, they reached a formidable 13.9% in the 2015 Spanish general elections.

How did they do it?

It is no exaggeration to say that Hervías was and still is on a frantic schedule. "I've been in my car, driving around in Spain, doing lots and lots of kilometres." He mentioned that for our interview, he had arrived the previous night from Santiago de Compostela in Galicia. Later on that day, he would continue his journey by taking a train to Seville. "I have been hands on doing that for the last few years" he said.

When Ciudadanos really started to get going on the national level, in 2014, the organisation was just him and an intern. He designed a 5-year expansion strategy in three phases. He planned to leave in 2019, after building a coherent and solid structure for the party, in each region of Spain.

They began by organising events across Spain. "I was meeting everybody. First of all open assemblies, open conversations in which everybody can participate. I would take note of the people who were participating most and of their abilities and skills. I tried to meet them one-to-one, to assess their talents, their particular abilities, where they could fit, what they could do, their interests and so on. That was it—basically personal contact."

He and others at the executive level stuck with the party. He thinks this continuity was a success factor, but acknowledged that continuous change is of the essence, at both regional and national levels: "The party wants teams to be led by the best possible people; the most talented, people who can really do things. So the objective is that the right people are in the right place to lead those teams by the time of the local and regional elections in 2019. And that's exactly what we are doing now. I have been doing the rounds; that's why I came from Galicia yesterday and am going to Andalucía today. We are changing the regional teams right now, and changing the leadership in some cases, so that by the time we get to 2019, everything is in place."

10.3 Scaling Strategy

If scaling can make or break a political start-up, what's the right way to do it? How do political entrepreneurs avoid making potentially existential mistakes?

"I'd be lying if I said I had the patent remedy for that," said Beate Meinl-Reisinger, at the time of our interview Chairwoman of NEOS Vienna, and since June, 2018 the Chairwoman of NEOS. "It is very clear; if you don't run in elections, you cannot build up a regional organisation. To take root, you need elections. Of course, ideally you get a good result. But you need the dynamic of a campaign to build up structures, and without structures it just doesn't work."

Does this simply mean you must compete in every election? Not necessarily. But there is strong incentive to do so, and therefore a built-in bias for political start-ups to try. After all, at the national level you only have one shot every 4 or 5 years.

Precisely because of this bias, NEOS has decided to counterbalance the political compulsion to enter all races with a key performance indicator (KPI)-based approach to scaling. Regional organisations must deliver against a set of KPIs before they can expect the endorsement of their contest by the Extended Board, the highest strategic institution of NEOS.

Those KPIs include benchmarks for amount of funding, number of candidates and of supporters, media appearances and other categories agreed between the federal and the regional organisation. The regional organisation needs to demonstrate it is up for the task by achieving agreed milestones in the respective dimensions. There is a 12-, 9- and 6-month deadline where the KPIs get reviewed. This leaves enough time to pull the plug on a hopeless endeavour before the point of no return, but it also leaves the regional organisation enough time to get back on track. Perhaps most importantly, it is a basis for mutual, fact-based expectations management, at a time when emotions may run high.

Scaling is not only a challenge to be grappled with beforehand. It also needs to be dealt with circumspectly once it has been successfully implemented. The new level or branch of the organisation needs to re-integrated into the whole, quickly and securely. Conflicts that may have been suppressed during the campaign must now be brought to the surface and resolved. A stock-take is needed. Mutual expectations need to be re-aligned accordingly. On the upside, a healthy and aligned regional organisation can give the whole a huge positive boost; on the downside, a rogue regional organisation can do enduring damage. Meinl-Reisinger knows this needs to be prevented, by design as much as by leadership: "To build up local and regional organisations is crucial, but those people have to feel obligated to act in the common interest, through their function, or at least by moral pressure."

But the obligations need to be reciprocal: "At the same time, if you want people to act, you need to give them power. I think we as an organisation oscillate between 'yes, let them do it, they have the damned duty to do it themselves' and 'I would like to control everything'. And that is an enormous balancing act. Without parameters it doesn't work, but having too many parameters gets people frustrated, particularly if they are volunteers."

Returning to organisation design (see Chap. 6), the balancing act can only work if the organisation is designed as a kind of hybrid, with a hierarchy on the one side, in the form of line and matrix management, and one the other, a network logic for operations. A hybrid design allows decentralised units that have the power to act, to be kept within the orbit of the mother ship; a hybrid between a start-up, a civic movement, and a political party.

10.4 In Opposition

Getting into Government straight away, as En Marche has managed, is the exception for political start-ups. At the time of writing, Ciudadanos, NEOS and Nowoczesna are all in opposition on national level, either for the first or the second term.

The experience being in opposition varies with the context. Nowoczesna quickly rose to being leader of the opposition, profiting from a weak Civic Platform, and from the fire they drew from the government. They held this position rather stable for a year, underlining it with tireless parliamentary work, and strong appearances in public. However, some, including its founder Ryszard Petru, believe Nowoczesna rose perhaps too quickly, and was unable, because of a lack of financial resources, to back up polls and growth with a professional organisation. And mistakes were made, as they always are. A political start-up is punished all the more if it disappoints the hopes people invest in it.

At the time of writing, Nowoczesna had stabilised around 5% in the polls, below its 2015 result of 7.6%. After an all-time high, the right-wing Law and Justice Party's momentum seemed to be stalling and the centre-right Civic Platform was on the rise again, reclaiming its role as leader of the opposition. Nowoczesna, under its new Chairwoman Katarzyna Lubnauer, had forged an alliance with the Civic Platform for the local elections in late 2018. It wasn't clear at the time of writing whether this strategic partnership would challenge the rule of PiS.

NEOS experienced a similar change of fortune. After the splash it made in the media following its surprising entry into parliament in 2013, it was starved of public interest as a 5% opposition party in parliament with no formal leverage. That did not deter the organisation from investing an enormous amount of energy in its parliamentary work. Perhaps a bit too much. "I saw the effort our MPs were putting into the committee work" Veit Dengler recalled. "Very impressive, but unfortunately useless in a political system like Austria's. They were proud of being the most diligent parliamentarians, so I asked them: how many votes have you won last month? And the answer to that was zero of course, because parliament proceedings in Austria are out of the public eye."

Dengler would have liked to require the MPs to spend a significant amount of time each week in the regions. But for a long time, NEOS did too little to involve its representatives in the local councils. Some became like organisational orphans. "To me" Dengler said, "the difference between the 5% party that NEOS is, and the 20% it could be, is this back-breaking work in the regions."

But NEOS did earn a good reputation as a serious and dedicated parliamentary force that was in for the long haul. The other newcomer in 2013, Team Stronach, crashed and burned a couple of years later, but NEOS kept its act together.

This helped to lay the groundwork for its success at the following election in 2017. Instead of being wiped out like the Greens, NEOS grew. In contrast to the first term, it also found itself in a position of formal leverage, as the holder of the balance of the constitutional two thirds-majority, which the two parties in government did not quite command between them.

In 2018, with its four elections on state-level, NEOS had the opportunity to branch out further across Austria, and put a strong focus on regional development. It managed to enter 3 out of 4 regional parliaments, and became part of its first Government coalition in Salzburg.

Ciudadanos were somewhat surprised themselves by their very strong result of 13.9% at their first showing in the Spanish general election in 2015. However, they managed to hold their own, and at the next general election the following year, lost less than one percentage point, to achieve 13.1%. "I think that Ciudadanos brought a new way of doing politics in Spain" said Vicente Rodrigo, a political scientist. "We were used to having very negative opposition parties. For the first time in history we had a constructive partner, Ciudadanos, that was not in the government, but was willing to build on proposals and policies, rather just criticise and point out what was bad."

The larger proposals and policies it presents are not only scrutinised internally, but also calculated in terms of costs and benefits. "I think we are the only stupid party in Europe that presents a supporting document to explain the numbers behind our core policies on a routine basis. We try to do that with every big initiative," explained Toni Roldán Monés, Ciudadanos' Director of Programme.

But Ciudadanos does not have all the answers, according to one of its parliamentary advisers, Jorge Lobeto: "Because we are not the government, we don't have to have answers for every problem in the country. We have to convey confidence and to demonstrate our ability to do things."

Ciudadanos uses its time in parliament to build up this capability, by backing it up with expertise: "We are in the second stage of getting into government", Roldán

Monés told me: "so we do not only need candidates, we also need groups of experts and the best professional talent."

10.5   Develop an Ecosystem

In his excellent book,"Triumphs of Experience", the researcher and author George E. Vaillant develops a theory of male adult development ("Triumphs of Experience: The Men of the Harvard Grant Study", Belknap Press, 2015). His theory is based on the Harvard Grant study, the longest longitudinal study of human development ever undertaken. He identifies a particular stage in the lives of the participants. He calls it "generativity", which he defines as a clear capacity of the adult to guide unselfishly the next generation, and to create or nurture things that will outlast them.

The developmental psychologist Erik and his wife Joan Erikson, in their eight stages of psychosocial development, put "Generativity" at Stage 7, and contrast it with "Stagnation", the failure to find a way to contribute (W.W. Norton & Company, 1998).

Since political start-ups want to bring about systemic change, as organisations they face the developmental task of helping to create and nurture other organisations that will outlast them. In fact, *that* may be the essence of systemic change.

NEOS, for example, has created new, non-party, stakeholder platforms, such as "Talents Thrive" in education, to provide social start-ups in this field with a platform and networking opportunities. Also, since the creation of NEOS, some of the first generation people have moved on, and founded their own business or social start-ups. One example is Sindbad, the social start-up of Andreas Lechner, NEOS's "first employee", and former Managing Director of NEOS Vienna. Sindbad provides 13–15 year-old students with mentors for 2 years. These mentors, who can be students or young professionals, help their mentees to master the transition into their next educational stage. Their vision is that by 2021, every third student at the eighth grade has a mentor, and they are well on track to achieve that. In this way Lechner and his partners are working to bring about the change in education that NEOS is advocating. In a way, NEOS the start-up has begun to spawn spin-offs.

Such transformational and generative work at various levels of society that produces comprehensive systemic change takes time and may never be completed, but it is essential if political start-ups are serious about bringing about the changes they advocate.

10.6   Re-Enter

In politics, the second time is always the hardest. About a third of political start-ups fail at their second encounter with the voting booth, according to the research by Nicole Bolleyer (op. cit.).

There are various reasons for that. The most important one, perhaps, lies in the nature of political start-ups: they have no voter base. The first time, some voters will have voted for the party simply because it was new. But the newness factor falls away the second time around. Other voters might have voted for the political start-up out of protest. But at the next election, the protest voters may move on to another party. Therefore, it is normal that a political start-up will exchange about half of its voters between its first and second elections. That is what NEOS experienced in 2017. So if you made 5% the first time, you cannot count on more than half of those people voting for you the second time. With a 4% threshold, that is not enough to get you back in.

Add to that the dynamics of the political market. While traditional parties may have been slow to learn historically, the time between two elections gives them enough breathing space to catch up and adapt. In Austria, for example, they did not only change their leaders (in the case of the ÖVP twice) between the two elections in 2013 and 2017, to field two much stronger candidates, who both appealed to the NEOS electorate. The ÖVP also radically changed its appearance, and upgraded its campaigning operations to a best practice model.

Finally, there's election dynamics. For any small party, including political start-ups, it always gets uncomfortable when the large parties fall out over who will be the Prime Minister. In the case of Austria in 2017, it turned into a three-way fight, with the right-wing Freedom party also seen to be a contender for the office. Such a "Lagerwahlkampf" (a fight between electoral camps) can lead to a crowding out of the smaller parties. This is what happened to the Austrian Greens in 2017: they lost voters to the Social Democrats, who wanted to prevent a national-conservative Government. In addition, they lost to NEOS and to the "Liste Pilz", the start-up of a Green MP who had split from the Greens. After being in Parliament for 31 years, they did not return in 2017.

NEOS did a lot of things right, committed no big mistakes, and attained 5.3%, gaining 0.3% and one MP, in very difficult circumstances. It is so far the first independently founded political start-up of a Western democracy to have managed to increase its vote at its second general election.

Again, success had a lot to do with Kairos (gaining momentum at the right time). It started with a major speech by NEOS Chairman Matthias Strolz at the end of May, 2017. This had actually been scheduled before anyone knew there would be an early election, but the timing was perfect. Once the elections were announced, the event was quickly transformed into a campaign launch. Strolz presented his book on his vision of a "Free Society of Opportunities". It not only provided NEOS with a societal narrative; it also transmitted a strong, vibrant signal at a crucial time. Some 700 people came to hear Strolz talk. The event also generated important imagery. One TV station broadcast his speech live.

This was followed by lots of media coverage, thanks to a series of "Opportunity Papers", that were endorsed and jointly presented by well-known and highly reputable public figures. The party's data analysis had also been much improved since 2013. The models had become much more precise, and had helped to target online and offline communication across Austria much more effectively.

Then the strategic alliance with Irmgard Griss was announced in July 2017, bringing the former presidential candidate on board as number two on the candidate list.

Most important of all, the management and the organisation of the campaign had improved. After many regional campaigns, there was now a lot of expertise on how to prepare, how to conduct, but also how to demobilise such a campaign the right way after an election. Consequently, there was much less drama. In the end, the two Campaign Managers Nick Donig and Claudia Jäger achieved a result to be proud of.

10.7 Getting into Government

On April 22, 2018, the state of Salzburg went to the polls. NEOS had not run in the previous election in 2013. It was only a few months before the 2013 parliamentary election, and the emerging political start-up did not have the resources for two campaigns. In consequence, the 2018 Salzburg election was the last one that NEOS contested for the first time. A cycle in the organisation's history was about to end.

The first half year of 2018 had been a busy one—in addition to Salzburg, there were state-level elections in Lower Austria, Carinthia and Tyrol, and a local one in Innsbruck, Austria's fifth largest city. Ultimately, with the exception of Carinthia, all of them proved to be successful for NEOS.

On election day, NEOS candidates, activists and the media gathered on the Mönchsberg, a mountain overlooking Salzburg, in the restaurant and bar M32, owned by gastronomer and restauranteur Sepp Schellhorn, Chairman of NEOS Salzburg. As always, the excitement increased as the clock approached 5 pm, the time of the first exit poll. When the NEOS column finally shot up to over 7%, people started cheering, jumping, laughing and hugging.

A few hours later, when the preliminary result was announced, a by-now-familiar pattern emerged: the party of the Governor, in that case the conservative ÖVP, had won significantly, whereas the opposing Social Democrats had lost, and the Greens had suffered a heavy defeat. NEOS had reached 7.3%, the best result of any regional election to date, with a campaign that had mostly been conducted in-house, without the support of an external agency. In the Parliament, that translated to three seats out of 36, on par with the Greens. That meant the coalition between the ÖVP and the Greens was history. It also meant that a three-way coalition with NEOS was at least a mathematical possibility.

There had already been contacts between NEOS Salzburg and the ÖVP ahead of the election. "A kind of sounding out each other", was how Nick Donig, the General Secretary of NEOS who was involved in brokering the coalition deal, described it during our interview in May, 2018. But when asked, Governor Wilfried Haslauer had always called a potential three-way coalition "improbable".

As was customary after an election, the leader of the strongest party, the Governor, invited other parties for preliminary talks. "He was in a comfortable position" said Donig, "because he had three coalition options to choose from: the Social

Democrats, the right-wing Freedom party, and a three-way coalition with the Greens and NEOS. So we went into the preliminary talks, having prepared ourselves based on what we had heard about how they worked—for example, we brought a list of our core policies. And we had a very long preliminary talk"—so long, that NEOS negotiators reckoned the Governor saw a three-way coalition as a real option.

After the preliminary talk, the NEOS team realised there were two policy issues on which they might not have expressed their position clearly enough. "We had red lines there" said Donig, "and we needed to keep to them. So we followed up with a letter to clarify this." Since Governor Haslauer had never indicated a willingness to negotiate on these issues the NEOS negotiators assumed their flirtation with power was over.

On the contrary, it had just begun. The Governor's reply was: "We received the letter, understood, negotiations start on Tuesday". Apparently, from a political point of view, Governor Haslauer saw merit in a coalition with NEOS and the Greens. "From that point on it was clear that, even for him, back-pedalling would be difficult" Donig explained. "It had to work out. All three parties had an interest in the success of the talks." The ÖVP Salzburg wanted to show there was a feasible alternative to the coalition with the right-wing FPÖ at the federal level, the Greens were fighting for survival, and NEOS wanted to enter Government for the first time.

10.7.1 Talking Coalition

On April 26, 2018, 4 days after the election, the formal coalition talks began; 10 daily rounds of negotiation would be spread across 3 weeks. How does such a process work in practice?

"It works differently, depending on the respective configuration" said Donig. "And yes, the majority party sets the tone. In our case, one party had 40%, one had 9%, and one had 7%. As in the Government now, a relative strength of about 5: 1: 1. So there is a clear leader."

The NEOS negotiating team consisted of NEOS representatives of all levels. Sepp Schellhorn, Chairman of NEOS Salzburg, took the lead as chief negotiator. Donig was there on behalf of the federal organisation. The newly elected State representatives were also members of the team. A staff member acted as recorder, and, depending on the area, political advisors from the parliamentary group alternated with local politicians from Salzburg. "We wanted to have all relevant players on board, so that everyone could subscribe to the resulting government programme", said Donig.

For each round of negotiations, there was a thematic block. The Conservatives provided a draft for each block, as a basis for negotiation. This draft was already a fully-formulated text for a government programme. The Greens and NEOS then went through that draft on their own, and set out their red lines, demands and wishes.

Doing described the process.

"You sit at the table with 15–18 people: the party representatives, plus one expert for each of the parties, plus the recorders. And you work on the document, which is projected onto a gigantic screen. A group of 15 people sit there and draft a text. Does that sound strange? It certainly felt rather strange.

You go through it paragraph by paragraph. For example, the Conservatives would start and say 'This is the preamble for Nature Protection, are there any comments?', and we would then say whether something was missing, or what should be altered from our point of view.

With the exception of the thematic block on Nature Protection, which took us much longer than planned, we always stayed on schedule. The days were divided up in blocks of four to five hours, like 9am-1pm and 2pm-6pm."

The result was an 82-page government programme.

I asked Doing whether there was ever a substantial issue in the negotiations where he thought they wouldn't work out after all.

"There were issues like that with the Greens, particularly around Nature Protection. There was a current problem, with wolves killing sheep. The Greens wanted to address the problem through a Government programme, but that did not make sense to us. So the three of us sat down. The representative of NEOS, which was known to be good with processes, suggested we take the wolves issue out of the negotiations, and instead allow the Greens to hold a press conference, where they could set out their position, and so separate the issue from the Government talks."

There were other issues where there was substantial disagreement among the three parties, but at the same time a willingness to trade them off against others. Those were put on a 'mutual bargaining list' that was negotiated at the very end. "For example, because every Euro was vital to them the Greens had a hard time accepting our demand on party subsidies. So we said, 'you got the wolves, so give us this one'."

Personnel and departmental decisions were discussed at the very end. "As the smaller party in Government, with only one department, you don't need that much creativity compared to staffing five or six," said Donig grinning. "Again, the majority party had clear ideas on how the Government should be structured, but they were open for discussion and negotiation. There was also rivalry between the two smaller parties, particularly on who got responsibility for integration. We won that one."

10.8 Challenges Ahead

After the coalition got underway, Donig saw various challenges facing NEOS and NEOS Salzburg. He differentiated between those specific to Salzburg, and those NEOS encounters each time it scales on the national level. "The one specific to Salzburg was that for a long time, we only had a city-based organisation there. It was certainly one of the strongest entities within NEOS, but now we have five strong entities, including a group in the State Parliament, a Second President of the State Parliament, and of course a State Secretary. So the cooperation and coordination between all the organisations and institutions on federal, the state and the city level, and forming them into 'One NEOS', certainly needs a lot of work."

More generally, as in other states of Austria, "our electoral success does not change the fact that we still have not arrived and have no structures in most of the towns of Salzburg. And on state level, we need to build up similar structures to the ones we have developed over the past 5 years at the federal level. So we need to tackle that next."

And then, of course, they need to prepare for the next election. "From the state's perspective, local elections are next, and then again the regional elections in 5 years—but now the federal organisation comes in and says, well, we also have a European election coming up, and elections for the Students Council, and the Economic Chamber... also, there might be elections in a bordering state, and we need to help each other, especially now, when we have a State Secretary who can also report on her experiences outside her home-state."

Donig sees Salzburg as a test-tube for future NEOS-involvement in government. "The question we always face is—what is of more benefit to us? Being the opposition, or going into Government? To get into Government, you of course have to make compromises. In such an uneven balance of power, as in the case of Salzburg, you risk being dubbed a tool, a junior in a supporting role, by the media as much as by the political competition. You get bruised for, in our case, accepting the role of the Second President of the State Parliament, which a larger opposition party would find unacceptable."

But Donig doesn't think NEOS had to make painful compromises in Salzburg. In his view, the decision to enter Government was better for Salzburg and for democracy as a whole, because the alternative was a right-wing Government with the Freedom party. It was also better for NEOS, he is convinced: "To be able to prove that we can also govern, that is a very important step for us. And, honestly, it is easier to try and test that at state level, than at the federal level."

Doing knows you cannot enter the same river twice, and that the next coalition talks will be different: "You do not get to claim the newbie bonus the second time around. People found it charming that we did not bring thousands of papers to the table, and refreshing that we involved lots of young advisors from the Parliament who were not necessarily that well versed with state law. We may not lose that altogether, but we will still need comprehensive programmes at state level that we do not have yet. So we will need to invest there. We don't need it for the campaign; we need it for what happens afterwards in the Coalition talks."

Donig is also acutely aware that HR and personnel development remains a challenge for NEOS. "We haul people into positions of responsibility almost overnight; political representatives as much as executive staff. So far we have not prepared ourselves well enough for that, and there is not yet a large enough talent pool to tap into. At the moment it is more like—we have two people for two positions, and both of them will have to do this for the first time."

That challenge only grows when you enter Government: "It accelerates you from 0 to 100. You need to take decisions that will be effective for the next 5 years. Suddenly you have 100 staff standing in front of you, who you're responsible for; 80 of them urgently want to talk to you, because they want to know where things go from here and whether their contracts will be extended."

10.9   Passing the Baton

Enoch Powell, one of Britain's most brilliant and controversial politicians, is best known for establishing immigration as a political issue in British politics. But he was also a great orator and a perceptive observer of the political game. In his biography of Joseph Chamberlain he said: "All political lives, unless they are cut off in midstream at a happy juncture, end in failure, because that is the nature of politics and of human affairs" (Thames and Hudson, 1977).

It has become almost a commonplace that the vast majority of politicians find it hard to relinquish the power political office provides, and at some point are either voted out of office by the electorate (e.g. Gerhard Schröder), or ousted by their own party (e.g. Margaret Thatcher). But there are exceptions. In the following pages, I present one case of a political life that involuntarily ended in failure, and another that was voluntarily cut off, or paused, at "a happy juncture".

As with any start-up, the handover of power from the founder of a political start-up to the next generation is a critical event. If it goes badly, it can threaten the very existence of the organisation. If it goes well, it can stimulate growth, and form the foundation for the party's next stage.

Start-ups often become over-dependent on their founders. An organisation steps into this founder's trap when it does not care enough about its pipe-line of new talent and fresh ideas. This can come back to haunt it later, when the founder leaves, and exposes a headless organisation, or the founder becomes a bottleneck restricting the organisation's development, and has to be forced out, as are 80% of founder-CEOs, according to Noam Wassermann ("The Founder's Dilemma", Harvard Business Review, 2008).

On November 25, 2017, Nowoczesna held its party congress in Warsaw. Two and a half years after its founding, leadership elections were due. The party had been on a roller-coaster ride since the beginning of the year. The private trip to Portugal of party founder and Chairman Ryszard Petru and his colleague Joanna Schmidt during the parliamentary crisis in December, 2016 had sent Nowoczesna into a tailspin. It dropped from 15 to 5% in the polls, before starting to recover to 8–10%.

Tensions, however, were again building up before the party congress. Just a few days earlier, Petru had announced a coalition between Nowoczesna and the conservative Civic Platform for the Mayoral election in Warsaw. He told supporters the party would not be running its own candidate for Mayor, but would support the Civic Platform candidate. But he had not consulted any of the relevant people in Warsaw, who had been campaigning for Nowoczesna's candidate for mayor, Pawel Rabiej, for many months, before his announcement. Warsaw accounted for 10% of the whole of Nowoczesna's membership. Moreover, it was not Petru's decision to make. According to Nowoczesna's constitution, it was up to the regional party to take the decision the party's Chairman had taken on their behalf. Although the Coalition with Civic Platform was later validated and broadened, the lack of communication was a disaster. People were disappointed, and angry.

The public were also unhappy with Nowoczesna's performance. In July, 2017, there had been a major protest against the judiciary reform plans of the Government.

Nowoczesna was very active, and again approached 10% in the polls. But from August, they started to sink again. And when they held focus groups, it emerged that the Chairman was part of that problem. Petru had been highly popular when he founded Nowoczesna in 2015, but two and a half years later he was no longer seen as a good and trustworthy leader. Some board members started to feel that they needed to bring about some visible change.

But Petru was still expected to win the leadership contest in November. He faced four challengers. Two were party heavy-weights: Nowoczesna's most high-profile MP, Kamila Gasiuk-Pihowicz, who had been in open conflict with Petru for a while, and Katarzyna Lubnauer, leader of the parliamentary group. Lubnauer had co-authored Nowoczesna's manifesto and had been deputy Chairman of the party since 2016. In April 2017, following the slump in the polls, she had also taken over the leadership of the parliamentary group. Petru had stayed on as party leader and the two had worked closely together thereafter.

"I decided late to become a candidate for party leader" she told me when we talked via Skype in June, 2018 "a week before the election. I did not campaign—I just phoned some people. It was difficult, because I had co-operated with Ryszard."

At the party congress, the first round of votes wasn't decisive. Lubnauer approached her rival, Kamila Gasiuk-Pihowicz, now Chief of the parliamentary group, and asked for her support. Gasiuk-Pihowicz agreed. "So I got her votes too, and I won." The final result was 149 for Lubnauer, and 140 for Petru.

Why did she win? "I won, because I was safe for the party", Lubnauer thinks. People knew her, what she could do, what she stood for. "The risk was low in picking me."

To many delegates, it was a sensation, to others, most of all to Petru himself, it came as a shock. After all, he was the party founder. Following the congress, Lubnauer asked him for a meeting. He said he would need time to think about the situation, and his future. He went to Amsterdam, to the annual ALDE congress. He returned 2 weeks later, went on television, and attacked Lubnauer. Although he had been elected to the party board "he did everything to make our situation worse", according to Lubnauer.

In January, Petru formed a new association, "Plan Petru", with the goal of bringing people from various opposition parties together, to discuss major issues, such as the Eurozone. He held country-wide meetings, under the Plan Petru-banner, using Nowoczesna party structures. Many in the party saw this as the embryo of a new political start-up he was planning. Again, the public took notice. "Everyone saw we were quarrelling within the party. When I began as the new leader, we were polling at around 10%. But in February, we began to sink again, because of the conflict between the former and the present leaders."

Lubnauer also had to face up to the fact that only about a third of the parliamentary group had voted for her, and that some regions had opposed her. She quickly organised meetings across the country. "The first thing I did after winning: I went to the regions which had voted against me." The listening campaign was a success, but the problems were far from over.

In May, Joanna Schmidt and Joanna Scheuring-Wielgus left the parliamentary group. A few days later, Petru followed. He told journalists that although Nowoczesna was his child, it was now going its own way, and he was unwilling to take responsibility for a party "over which I have no influence." ("Founder of Poland's opposition party Nowoczesna quits", Radio Poland, May 11, 2018). At the time of writing, Petru is planning to found a new "social liberal party".

Since her election in November, 2017, Lubnauer has avoided a party split, begun an internal reconciliation, kept the party together despite a public confrontation with its now departed founder, and started to transform Nowoczesna from a founder-focused start-up into an effective team. And, so far, the coalition with Civic Platform seems promising.

But it is clear that the road ahead remains rocky. At the time of writing, Nowoczesna is polling 4–6%, well below the 7.6% achieved in 2015. Fall-out from the acrimonious handover of power has added to the challenges of a political start-up that had been polling as the strongest opposition party for the whole of 2016. Re-entering the Polish Parliament by crossing the 5% threshold in Autumn, 2019 is within reach, but by no means assured.

On a sunny Sunday afternoon in May, 2018 friends visited my wife and I in our apartment in Vienna. We had not met in a while, so we updated each other on private and professional matters. When the question of how NEOS was doing came up, I said "fine, thank you. We had a by and large successful first half of the year, entering three of four possible regional governments." And then I added: "now the election season is over, things are calming down a bit."

Twelve hours later, on May 7, NEOS Chairman Matthias Strolz told me on the phone that he would resign, and hand over both the party and the parliamentary group in a structured, step-by-step process by the end of the year.

What took me by surprise (I had expected the move in 2019), came as a shock to the organisation. What the heck had just happened? As was always the case with Strolz, an orchestrated communication process kicked off immediately. Within a very short period of time, he informed all relevant stakeholders about his decision—first the strategic bodies, staff, the members, and then the public. In reality, what we saw unfold in front of our eyes were the consequences of a decision he had taken at the end of 2017. In the following months, he had prepared the handover meticulously, and wrote it down in a 40-page document plus additional material he had started to draft in April, 2018.

Only a handful of people had been in the loop: his wife, Irene, his sister, and his long-time personal assistant, Sena Beganovic. A few days before the announcement he had talked with Beate Meinl-Reisinger, his deputy and Chairwoman of NEOS Vienna. He saw her as the person best suited to take over, and wanted to make sure that she was ready. Once she gave him the green light, he went ahead.

Almost immediately, there was speculation in the media. What were the *real reasons* behind this bold step? Why did the popular politician step down in his prime? After all, NEOS was just about to enter its first Government coalition in Salzburg. On the federal level, according to several journalists, Strolz was the perceived leader of the opposition. Why now? Was he ill? Had he had an affair? Was it a #metoo issue? Was a fourth child on the way?

None of the above, Strolz clarified in a blog post he published the same afternoon. It was simply "the right time for the next step" (*Kairos*, once again). NEOS had arrived at the end of its start-up phase. Salzburg was the last election that NEOS had fought for the first time. Every election that followed, NEOS would have contested at least once. It was becoming a more settled, more professional organisation. It was getting ready for its next growth spurt, and he saw the skills of others, Meinl-Reisinger's in particular, better suited for the challenges of the next stage. He wanted to prevent NEOS from falling into the "founder's trap".

And finally, apart from these organisational considerations, he had never intended to stay in politics for more than 10 years. He had a professional life before politics, and he certainly planned to have one after. "I am not the passenger, but the pilot of my own life" he wrote in the blog, in an oft-quoted passage.

Even after some long interviews, speculation in the media about the *real reasons* did not fully abate. It was simply unheard of for a politician to leave the political arena for good, without being defeated at the polling booth or being brought down by some kind of scandal, or internal back-stabbing.

Although his decision to quit left some citizens disappointed and even angry, the overwhelming majority of the public were very positive about it. Strolz himself estimated the reactions to be 80% positive, and 20% disappointed or angry. His numbers were soon corroborated by a regular survey of public trust in politicians, where he rose to second place, behind Chancellor Sebastian Kurz. He had gone some way towards answering the question posed in his 2011 book "Why we don't trust politicians, and what they (would) have to do to change that".

A couple of weeks after his announcement, I asked Matthias whether he thought that things had gone according to script. He said things had actually gone better than in the script. The process was still underway at the time of writing, but so far things have gone really well at NEOS. After the first shock, the organisation rose to the occasion, and dealt effectively with all the consequences.

Political Entrepreneurs and the Evolution of Democracy

Democracy isn't broken, as some on the left and right claim, but not even its most ardent advocates would claim it is a picture of health at the end of the second decade of the twenty-first century. It is suffering from multifactorial disorders, which, if left untreated, could inflict serious damage on the body politic. Fortunately, democracy has self-healing properties. Its illness has mobilised its immune system, and antigens in the persons of centrist political entrepreneurs are on the march.

If democracy is to evolve, so must political parties. In their pure form, traditional parties and political start-ups are two poles of one continuum. They are designed differently, they act differently, and they *feel* different. While traditional parties are creatures of the twentieth century (some were even created in the nineteenth century), political start-ups are children of the twenty-first. In what ways do they differ from one another?

Eric Ries, in his book "The Start-up Way" (Crown Business, 2017), suggests some ways to distinguish between "old-fashioned" and "modern" companies, which I have adapted for political start-ups (Table 11.1).

11.1 Political Intrapreneurship

Is the above logic really strictly binary—can an organisation only be either of the two? Can only political start-ups act entrepreneurially?

I don't think so, which is why I called it a "continuum" with two poles. Political logic and mechanisms force political start-ups to become more like traditional parties over time. Working against becoming just one more party takes conscious effort. It is like working against entropy: if you do not adapt and re-integrate *all the time*, you will soon be like most of the others: dead.

That implies that traditional parties can become more like political start-ups. In fact there are examples where traditional parties were forced to evolve into start-ups, like the FDP in Germany, which was thrown out of the Bundestag at the national

© Springer Nature Switzerland AG 2019
J. Lentsch, *Political Entrepreneurship*,
https://doi.org/10.1007/978-3-030-02861-9_11

Table 11.1 The political zoo

Traditional party	Political enterprise
Hold on to what you got	Think big, start small, scale fast
Protected from competition via barriers to entry	Leaves competitors in the dust through continuous learning and experimentation
Re-organises policy platforms and organisational structures once in a decade	Has everything in permanent beta
Organically grown	Co-designed
Composed of party managers and their subordinates	Composed of leaders and empowered political entrepreneurs
HR as yearly appraisal	HR as core function to identify, attract, develop and retain political entrepreneurs on all levels
Politics as career	Politics as project
Diffused accountability	Individual accountability
Line management	Line, matrix and project-based management
Opaque	Transparent
Fragmented structures	Highly integrated structures
Organised along departmental and sectional silos	Consists of cross-functional teams that work together to serve voters through iterative and scientific processes
Few or no experiments	Operates rapid experiments all the time
Digital as a department	Digital embedded in everything
Data-based	Data-driven
Stakeholder management	Generative, fosters creation of innovative eco-systems

Based on Ries (2017)

election in 2013, and had to fight its way back, by becoming more entrepreneurial, agile and digital. The required radical reforms were pushed by "intrapreneurs". In the business world, this term was coined to describe people who create innovation within an existing, often larger organisation. Such people can be found in the political world as well.

Traditional parties, however, with all their vested interests and multiple power logics, often find it hard to innovate, if there is no clear and present danger to their existence. After all, they are about *power*. This is why there are few examples of genuinely successful transformations of traditional parties, and a legion of failed efforts. At their best, they often amount to no more than rearranging the deck chairs on the *Titanic*.

How, then, could you transform a traditional party into something like a new political enterprise? A comprehensive answer to this question is beyond the scope of this book, but a practical place to start would be to try to apply some of the tools and insights presented here. And a good place to experiment with them and run pilots would be politically "underdeveloped" areas with growth potential. New communal and regional off-shoots of parties can be viewed as political start-ups themselves. Here, the same logic applies: "Start small. Think big. Scale fast." The central challenge, however, is the "scale fast" part: to make experimental reforms success-ful, some internal rules and structures may have to be altered, which may disrupt the organisation as a whole. And this is the adaptive challenge where most traditional parties hit the brakes. They are reluctant to open "Pandora's Box", because to do so would mean altering the existing internal power structure.

But the stark fact remains that traditional centrist political parties, social democrats on the centre left and conservatives on the centre right, are in a crisis. As Chicago Mayor Rahm Emanuel said: "Never let a good crisis go to waste". The burning platform may prove a sufficient threat to counter the resistance to profound change in traditional parties, but I have yet to find evidence of that. Until I do, I shall remain a firm believer that Political Entrepreneurship is the best hope for our political future.

11.2 Political Entrepreneurship in the UK and the US

In the UK, the formation of a new centrist party appeared to be underway at the time of writing ("New centrist party gets £50m backing to 'break mould' of UK politics", Michael Savage, The Guardian, April 8, 2018). And there was talk of another one or two in the preparatory stages. It would certainly not be the first, and most probably would not be the last political start-up to try to disrupt the Tory-Labour duopoly of British politics.

Over the past couple of years, I have had arguments about the possibility of Political Entrepreneurship in first-past-the-post (FPTP) democracies such as the UK and the US. These "winner takes all" systems favour the development of two large parties; the Tories and Labour in the UK; the Republicans and Democrats in the US. Third parties rarely play important roles in peacetime. There are exceptions (like the Lib-Lab pact in 1977–1978 and the LibDems in the Cameron-Clegg coalition from 2010 to 2015), but the major parties generally take turns to govern. The minor parties remain on the electoral fringes.

"Look at history" my opponents would insist. "FPTP is too hard for third parties". The Green party in the US, the Social Democrats in the UK—they were both driven by passion and good intentions, but in the end they became irrelevant. In the end, they failed. I agree that it is extremely hard. If getting to scale is a super tough hurdle in proportional representation systems, it must be almost insurmountable in FPTP systems, and becoming sustainable thereafter would be even more difficult.

But, as I have tried to show throughout this book, we live in extraordinary times. We live in the time of Brexit, where both the Tories and Labour seem to have become dysfunctional and toxic. We live in the age of Trump, where many Republicans seem to have rejected the virtues of moderation and decency, and where Democrats seem to be in a perpetual state of mourning for what might have been.

In such extraordinary times, extraordinary things become possible. In fact, they are necessary. History provides examples of occasions when a new party disrupts a dysfunctional political market, even in FPTP systems. The US Republican party was created in 1854 by anti-slavery activists, economic modernisers and liberal Whigs.

The party dominated politics nationally and in most northern states for most of the period between 1860 and 1932.

More than 160 years later, we are again at a point of high electoral volatility, where whole political systems can reach a cusp point and flip to a very different setup very quickly; just look at France, and the country most likely to change its political setup next, Spain. Observers in the US and particularly the UK will watch the developments in Europe with interest. If such a political start-up can make significant headway in the UK, the United States will be next in line for a centrist revolution.

11.3   The Trouble with Democracy

What ails democracy these days, according to the social scientist and philosopher Harald Katzmair, is that parties are more complex, harder and more expensive to manage, and thus less agile and variable: "That leads to highly centralised power structures that are less and less capable of using the knowledge produced on the periphery and semi-periphery, and less and less capable of being in tune with it."

Katzmair, who advised Barack Obama's campaign during the 2008 US election, is a great fan of the political periphery and semi-periphery, because that's where true novelty and innovation come from. "We know from research" he told me when I interviewed him in January 2018, "that those at the centre of networks have the least freedom to enter new relationships. Why? Because for someone to become Prime Minister, for example, he or she had to enter at least five mutual dependency relationships that he or she needs to honour."

This lack of freedom at the top means the new ideas the system needs to renew itself can't reach the centre, and those on the periphery can't align themselves with the centre. "So what you get" said Katzmair "is a political system that loses its coherence and learning ability. Instead of going to the roots of problems, politics gets focused more on more on symptoms, and cultural arguments."

The failure to address the real issues undermines public trust in politics. People tend to see democracy as the rule of the majority, but that's the authoritarian version. In a representative democracy the majority decides on the institutions through which the various parts of the electorate negotiate compromises. This is how what Katzmair calls the "general will", which doesn't exist in the first place, is constructed. For a political party to begin to address the real issues, and construct the general will, its centre must be connected with its periphery.

That the two are usually not well connected in political parties is evident in a lack of horizontal social mobility. "We do not have many politicians who enter the private sector, many civil servants entering academia, or academics entering politics, and so on", Katzmair explained. "That is the effect of ever more concentrated systems. In an up-or-out logic, the centre orients everything towards itself. You get selection games in the various segments around the centre, and those who make it get admitted. So you destroy any horizontal mobility within the periphery, because everyone is looking to get into the centre."

One Party, Many Places

The solution, according to Katzmair, is to strengthen the periphery's self-organising capabilities, and the autonomy that comes with that. "That's how US mega-churches are structured" said Katzmair. "One church—many places." Small groups come first and are aligned with the centre through training, and regular services. It's a cellular model. The local group model, with lots of small decentralised units, is in Katzmair's opinion, "the only way to build movements that do not immediately implode. Online pirate movements that don't embed themselves in the daily lives of people come and go. But if you want to embed the party in the daily routines of people, and build it up, you need to organise in that way. This is how we did it for the Obama campaign, with local groups where people met to socialise and talk politics. 'Promoting democracy—one beer at a time.' One church, many places."

Katzmair said that if democracy is be renewed, or reinvented "it needs a periphery long before we talk of a centre, or a vision of the future." He sees clubs and other small local associations and groups "not necessarily political ones—it can be cooking, healthy food, gardening, or whatever" as the essential proto-political building blocks of a movement.

The Loss of Synchronisation

The way Katzmair sees it, "the mass parties developed because the factory or the church provided a cultural imprint that synchronised people proto-politically. They left the factory at the same time, lived in the same housing block, owned the same car, and on Sunday they read the same newspaper. So there was this synchronisation of the living environment on which the political environment was built."

As our societies became increasingly diverse, we lost that synchronisation. "But now that synchronisation is provided by algorithms designed to minimise the cognitive dissonance, by connecting people with others like themselves and so minimising the Triple-A of anxiety, ambiguity and ambivalence. But to be able to compromise, and have a democracy in which people hand over power without violence, you need that Triple-A."

That's why he favours small groups, where people realise they see things differently, and yet share their lifetimes: "A new political movement must design itself along those lines."

"En Marche did it like that" I said. "Perfect" Katzmair replied. "And you can use that for political questions on the regional level, or as focus groups, or as a sounding boards, or whatever. But you have to leave their purposes up to them."

11.4   The Future of Political Entrepreneurship

As a movement, Political Entrepreneurship is in its infancy. In the coming years, the main challenge will be making it mainstream globally. The lessons learned from start-ups and the social enterprise movement suggest three key challenges must be addressed over the next few years.

Empowering Political Entrepreneurs at all Levels
The tools of Political Entrepreneurship could be made broadly accessible on- and offline via training courses.

A European and global Political Entrepreneurs Network could be established. Its function could be to celebrate successes and failures alike, and to cross-pollinate ideas and innovations. Ultimately, this could lead to a global movement of centrist political entrepreneurs.

The spreading of new and experimental types of regular open, and participative political conferences across Europe like the *European Forum Alpbach*, the *Innovation in Politics Awards*, the Creative Bureaucracy Festival, *Alter Ego, Open State of Politics* or *Innocracy* could help envision and embody new models of politics. They could also help match and connect political entrepreneurs.

Today's political entrepreneurs are more often male. A special effort should be made to empower female political entrepreneurs.

Building an Institutional Base
Like Ashoka, which has made investment in the concept of Social Entrepreneurship mainstream over the past 30 years, Political Entrepreneurship needs an organisation to act as its champion, in the same ways as the Impact Hub, with its global network of co-working spaces, acts as the champion of Social Entrepreneurs.

Non-governmental institutions could be created to provide early-stage seed-funding for political start-ups.

At the European level, Fellowships for political entrepreneurs and future political and civic leaders, similar to those awarded by the Truman Fellowship in the US, could be created.

The planned European Universities could offer applied executive programmes for political entrepreneurs.

An organisation analogous to social enterprise's "Teach First", possibly called "Serve First", could be created to support young people who want to run as candidates and serve as representatives at all levels of politics.

Incubators and accelerators could be formed for centrist political start-ups at all levels. The party academies and political foundations of current political start-ups could transform themselves accordingly, or develop prototypes and spin them off.

A Deeper Understanding of Political Entrepreneurship
The concept of Political Entrepreneurship, and particularly the under-researched field of *centrist* Political Entrepreneurship, should be refined by further research, and the subject of Political Entrepreneurship could be integrated into academic curricula.

Epilogue

A talent for speaking differently, rather than for arguing well is the chief instrument of cultural change.

Richard Rorty

I hope I have done justice to the thoughts and insights of my interviewees. It was great fun doing the interviews, and I sometimes caught myself laughing when I transcribed them, or incorporated them in the text. Fun is an undervalued resource in politics, and I hope that it shines through in this book. As Seneca said, true joy is a serious thing.

The emergence of centrist political start-ups is a new phenomenon and the language and the concepts for describing it are not yet fully developed. If I have not argued their case well, I hope at least, as Richard Rorty put in the above quote, that I have spoken for them differently.

But I have no doubt that the recently emerged phenomenon of the centrist political start-up is here to stay. Do I believe that they alone will save the world? No. It will take people of good-will in political parties old and new to bring about a true transformation of our ailing democratic systems in the twenty-first century.

The role of centrist political start-ups in this systemic transformation process is that of pioneers, catalysts and increasingly, of leaders. What differentiates them from traditional parties is not so much that they make fewer mistakes—they make plenty of them, arguably more—but how they learn from them.

Traditional parties can, and should, therefore learn from political start-ups. Perhaps some may regard this advice as the arrogance of the *parvenu*, but, as one interviewee put it: "you need a certain amount of arrogance to claim you will found a political start-up, defeat the parties in power, and transform the political system."

It is quite possible that the next political start-up to have a major impact will not be in continental Europe, but in the UK or the US. I know the conventional wisdom is that first-past-the-post systems are hostile environments for the emergence of significant new parties, but conventional wisdoms apply to the normal situation— and I think we are way past normal now.

© Springer Nature Switzerland AG 2019
J. Lentsch, *Political Entrepreneurship*,
https://doi.org/10.1007/978-3-030-02861-9

In the meantime, political start-ups such as those portrayed in this book will continue to grow, enter governments, change the political landscape, and yes, some of them will also fail. I salute them, and everyone engaged in them. Tomorrow it might be too late. It is time to make the change now.

Appendix

Table A.1 How political entrepreneurship works—a roadmap

Stage	Milestones	Tasks	Routes
Understand	Understanding political systems	• Understand rules of the system and key players • Identify system challenges and political market opportunities	• Work or volunteer in political periphery or adjacent field • Read • Interview • Publish book or blogs
Envision	Envisioning a new politics	• Formulate a substantiated vision of future political system, and critique of status quo • Test the waters	• Publish book or blogs • Take a deep personal dive • Formulate a manifesto
Build	Prepare	• Prepare yourself, and your immediate environment • Find sparring partners, mentors, accomplices, advisors, matrons/patrons and first followers • Interlink islands of discontent	• Identify trustful acquaintances who have something essential to contribute • Identify potential strategic partners, and relevant societal stakeholders • Establish small group of regulars
	Assemble	• Establish solid core group • Start crowd funding • Start continuously identifying and empowering talent	• Have everyone chip in • Identify the "right time" to mobilise a maximum number of the right people • Map out path and process to election • Organise first gathering
	(Co-)Design	• Co-design shared vision, mission and values • Prototype core manifesto • Prototype organisation design (strategy, culture, structure and processes) • Prototype brand design	• Conduct regular large-group workshops • Monitor attrition, be ready to on- and off-board regularly, with a focus on growth • Invite potential strategic partners

(continued)

Table A.1 (continued)

Stage	Milestones	Tasks	Routes
		• Consolidate and grow core group	
	Reach out, and road-test and reiterate	• Early-on feedback loops on core manifesto in the field • Recruit supporters • Build leadership team	• Conduct citizen forums with prototypes of core manifesto • Conduct a door-to-door campaign
	Build-up critical mass	• Raise your flag in the political arena • Get media attention	• Run (or run against) a petition • Focus on earned media • Build up owned media channels and database of contacts
	Launch	• Legally set-up political start-up • Go public • Endure systemic immune reaction	• Find founding board • Recruit founding members • Conduct impressive founding congress
	Build competitive capacity	• Do the math • Attract good people • Hire key staff • Build up competitive funding • Build up intelligence • Build strategic alliances • Recruit candidates • Recruit campaign team • Establish expert advisory group	• Go on tour • Recruit major donors • Do a petition • Go door-to-door • Load the contacts database • Base everything on data • Get a rebel base
	Run	• Target • Position • Communicate • Mobilise • Manage internal conflicts • Plan for contingencies	• Get outside help on strategy and planning (e.g. European parties and /or political consultancies) • Target based on data model • Position based on qualitative and quantitative research • Get everyone to give their all until the very last minute
	Enter	• Endure the hype • Resist the system • De-mobilise • Secure results • Re-integrate • Re-engage • Re-focus on external • Avoid rookie mistakes • Transition from feel-good start-up to professional organisation • Start consolidating financially	• Consciously design a process of workshops representative of all internal stakeholders • Draft an election handbook • Have some tough and honest conversations with volunteers and staff • Give time for the dust to settle before making strategic decisions

(continued)

Table A.1 (continued)

Stage	Milestones	Tasks	Routes
Scale	Scaling solutions	• Replicate • Grow support structure in line • Learn to say no • Keep unity in diversity • Build stakeholder platforms • Impact as opposition • Impact as party in government	• Use a kpi-based approach • Empower people in the regions • Run in regional elections • Be present in the regions
	Generate	• Generate an ecosystem of systems change	• Foster strategic outplacements • Support friendly spin-offs and newly founded enterprises by ex-staff
	Re-enter	• Build alliances • Account for results from previous campaign(s) • Broaden leadership base, and build up potential successor	• Keep organisation open • Be prepared to start from almost zero
	Govern	• Cultivate relations with potential coalition partners • Have an impact on the government programme • Keep all organisations aligned	• Work out full-fledged regional programme • Involve all relevant internal stakeholder in coalition talks
Hand over	Hand over	• Avoid founder's trap • Clear cut, structured process	• Script the process • Hand over when organisation is strong, and has no immediate elections coming up

Bibliography

Abel, François. "The Political Entrepreneur and the Coordination of the Political Process: A Market Process Perspective of the Political Market". Review of Austrian Economics 16/2–3, 153–168. 2003.

Alemanno, A. and Cottakis, M. "Why Europe Needs Civic Entrepreneurs." Social Europe. 10 November 2017. https://www.socialeurope.eu/why-europe-needs-civic-entrepreneurs. Accessed: 25 May 2018.

Baumol, William J. "Entrepreneurship: Productive, Unproductive, and Destructive". Journal of Political Economy. 1990. Vol. 98, No. 5, Part 1. https://www.colorado.edu/ibs/es/alston/econ4504/readings/Baumol%201990.pdf. Accessed: 25 May 2018.

Bolleyer, Nicole. "New parties in old systems". Oxford University Press. Oxford. 2013.

Bornstein, David. "How to Change the World: Social Entrepreneurs and the Power of New Ideas." Oxford University Press. Oxford. 2010.

Brooker, Katrina. "Airbnb's ambitious second act will take it way beyond couchsurfing". Vanity Fair. Nov 2016. https://www.vanityfair.com/news/2016/11/airbnb-brian-chesky. Accessed: 28 May 2018.

Brown, Archie. "The Myth of the Strong Leader: Political Leadership in the Modern Age." Basic Books. New York. 2014.

Burnett, Dean. "Why political parties fall apart: the psychology of infighting". The Guardian. 21 Mar 2016. https://www.theguardian.com/science/brain-flapping/2016/mar/21/ids-trump-corbyn-psychology-political-parties-infighting. Accessed: 28 May 2018.

Cohen, Peter. "Harvard's Lion of Entrepreneurship Packs Up His Office". Forbes.com. 15 June 2011. https://www.forbes.com/sites/petercohan/2011/06/15/harvards-lion-of-entrepreneurship-packs-up-his-office/#36d9d2f44e89. Accessed: 27 Aug 2018.

Collins, Jim. "Great by Choice". HarperBusiness. New York. 2011.

Dahl, Robert: "Who Governs? Democracy and Power in an American City." New Haven (Conn.): Yale University Press. 1961.

Dahl, Robert. "Democracy and its Critics." Yale University Press. New Haven. 1991.

Diamond, Larry. "Facing up to the Democratic Recession". Journal of Democracy. Volume 26/Issue 1. January 2015.

Dubéci, Martin & Filko, Martin. "Move on." https://www.progresivne.sk/en/move-on/. Accessed: 28 May 2018.

Duverger, Maurice. "Les partis politiques". Seuil. Paris. 1992.

Edelman. "2018 Edelman Trust Barometer". https://www.edelman.com/post/the-battle-for-truth. Accessed: 25 May 2018.

Eisenmann, Thomas R. "What is Entrepreneurship". Harvard Business Review. January/February 2013. https://hbr.org/2013/01/what-is-entrepreneurship. Accessed: 25 May 2018.

Freedom House. "Freedom in the World". 2018. https://freedomhouse.org/report/freedom-world/freedom-world-2018. Accessed 25 May 2018.

Friedman, Uri. "What if the 'Populist Wave' ist just political fragmentation?". The Atlantic. 17 Mar 2017. https://www.theatlantic.com/international/archive/2017/03/dutch-election-wilders-populism/519813/. Accessed: 28 May 2018.

© Springer Nature Switzerland AG 2019
J. Lentsch, *Political Entrepreneurship*,
https://doi.org/10.1007/978-3-030-02861-9

Foley, Michael. "Political Leadership: Themes, Contexts and Critiques". Oxford University Press. Oxford. 2013.

"Founder of Poland's opposition party Nowoczesna quits." Radio Poland. 11 May 2018. http://thenews.pl/1/9/Artykul/363047,Founder-of-Poland%E2%80%99s-opposition-Nowoczesna-party-quits. Accessed: 15 June 2018.

Garicano, Luis & Roldán, Antonio: "Recuperar el future". Península. Madrid. 2015.

Gendron, George. "Flashes of Genius". Inc. 15 May 1996. https://www.inc.com/magazine/19960515/2083.html. Accessed: 28 May 2018.

Gramsci, Antonio. "Selections from the Prison Notebooks". Orient Black Swan. Telangana. 1996.

Grant, Adam. "Originals: How Non-Conformists Move the World". Viking. New York. 2016.

Hederer, Christian. "Political entrepreneurship and institutional change: an evolutionary perspective". Paper prepared for EAEPE conference, Porto, November 2007. https://www.fep.up.pt/conferencias/EAEPE2007/Papers%20and%20abstracts_CD/Hederer.pdf. Accessed: 26 June 2018.

Holcombe, Randall. "Political Entrepreneurship and the Democratic Allocation of Economic Resources". The Review of Austrian Economics, vol. 15, issue 2–3, 143–59. 2002.

https://www.ashoka.org/en/focus/social-entrepreneurship. Accessed: 28 May 2018.

http://data.opendataportal.at/dataset?q=neos&sort=score+desc%2C+name+asc. Accessed: 28 May 2018.

https://opensource.com/open-source-way. Accessed: 28 May 2018.

Hug, Simon. "Studying the Electoral Success Of New Political Parties: A Methodological Approach". Party Politics. VOL 6. No. 2 pp. 187–197. 2000.

Ignatieff, Michael. "Fire and Ashes: Success and Failure in Politics". Harvard University Press. Cambridge. 2013.

International Institute for Democracy and Electoral Assistance. "The Global State of Democracy: Exploring Democracy's Resilience". 2017. https://www.idea.int/gsod/files/IDEA-GSOD-2017-PREFACE-EN.pdf. Accessed: 25 May 2018.

Kopraleva, Iva. "Are Pirate Parties relevant to European politics?" European Council on Foreign Relations. 20 Jan 2017. https://www.ecfr.eu/article/commentary_are_pirate_parties_relevant_to_european_politics_7221. Accessed: 15 June 2018.

Krastev, Ivan. "After Europe". Combined Academic Publishing. Harrogate. 2017.

Lago, Ignacio & Martínez, Ferran. "Why new parties?". Party Politics, Vol 17, Issue 1, pp. 3–20. 2010.

Leadbeater, Charles and Goss, Sue. "Civic Entrepreneurship". Demos. 1998. http://charlesleadbeater.net/wp-content/uploads/1998/01/Civicentrepreneurship.pdf. Accessed: 25 May 2018.

Levitsky, Steven & Ziblatt, Daniel. "How Democracies Die." Crown. New York. 2018.

Lovegrove, Nick and Thomas, Matthew. "Triple-Strength Leadership". Harvard Business Review. September 2013. https://hbr.org/2013/09/triple-strength-leadership. Accessed: 28 May 2018.

Luce, Edward. "The Retreat of Western Liberalism". Little, Brown. London. 2017.

Macron, Emmanuel. "Révolution". Xo Editions. Paris. 2016.

Martin, Roger L., and Osberg, Sally. "Getting beyond better". Harvard Business Review Press. Cambridge. 2015.

Mishra, Pankaj. "The Age of Anger". Allen Lane. London. 2017.

Mounk, Yascha. "The People vs. Democracy." Harvard University Press. Cambridge. 2018.

Petru, Ryszard & Lipiński, Łukasz. "Koniec wolnego rynku? Geneza kryzysu". NCK. Warsaw. 2014.

Powell, Enoch. "Joseph Chamberlain". Thames & Hudson. London. 1977.

Radosh, Roland. "Steve Bannon, Trump's Top Guy, Told me he was a 'Leninist'". The Daily Beast. 22 Aug 2016. https://www.thedailybeast.com/steve-bannon-trumps-top-guy-told-me-he-was-a-leninist. Accessed: 28 May 2018.

Reynié, Dominique (edr). "What next for Democracy?" Fondation pour l'innovation politique. Paris. 2017.

Robbins, Lionel. "The Theory of Economic Development in the History of Economic Thought." Macmillian. London and Basingstoke. 1968. https://mises.org/sites/default/files/The%20Theory%20of%20Economic%20Development_2.pdf. Accessed: 25 May 2018.

Sandner, Günther. "Otto Neurath: Eine politische Biografie." Zsolnay. Wien. 2014.

Savage, Michael. "New centrist party gets £50m backing to 'break mould' of UK politics". The Guardian. 8 Apr 2018. https://www.theguardian.com/politics/2018/apr/07/new-political-party-break-mould-westminster-uk-brexit. Accessed: 28 May 2018.

Scharmer, Otto. "Theory U: Learning from the Future as it emerges." Berrett-Koehler. Oakland. 2009.

Schneider, M. & Teske, P.: "Toward a Theory of the Political Entrepreneur: Evidence from Local Government". American Political Science Review 86: 737–747. 1992.

Schumpeter, Joseph. "Capitalism, Socialism and Democracy". Harper Perennial Modern Classics. New York City. 2008.

Schurenberg, Eric. "What's an Entrepreneur? The best answer ever." Inc. 9 January 2012. https://www.inc.com/eric-schurenberg/the-best-definition-of-entepreneurship.html. Accessed: 25 May 2018.

Seelos, Christian and Mair, Johanna. "Innovation and Scaling for Impact: How Effective Social Enterprises Do it." Stanford University Press. Palo Alto. 2017.

Sheingate, Adam D.: "Political Entrepreneurship, Institutional Change, and American Political Development." Studies in American Political Development 17: 185–203. 2003.

Stanford, Naomi. "Guide to Organisation Design." Profile Books. London. 2007.

Strolz, Matthias. "Warum wir Politikern nicht trauen: und was sie tun müss(t)en, damit sich das ändert." Kremayr & Scheriau. Wien. 2011.

The Economist. "The new political divide". 30 July 2016. https://www.economist.com/news/leaders/21702750-farewell-left-versus-right-contest-matters-now-open-against-closed-new. Accessed: 25 May 2018.

Thierry, Feri. "Aus dem Leben eines Parteigeschäftsführers". NEOS. 19 Feb 2014. https://partei.neos.eu/aus-dem-leben-eines-partei-geschaeftsfuehrers/. Accessed: 28 May 2018.

Thiel, Peter. "Zero to One". Currency. New York. 2014.

Vaillant, George. "Triumphs of Experience: The Men of the Harvard Grant Study." Belknap Press: An Imprint of Harvard University Press. Cambridge. 2015.

Wassermann, Noam. "The Founder's Dilemma." Harvard Business Review. February 2008. https://hbr.org/2008/02/the-founders-dilemma. Accessed: 28 May 2018.

Weber, Max. "The Vocation Lectures." Hackett Classics. Indianapolis. 2004.

Witter, Lisa & de Vries, Catherine. "Reclaiming Democracy: A Plea for Political Entrepreneurship". Stanford Social Innovation Review. 31 Oct 2013. https://ssir.org/articles/entry/reclaiming_democracy_a_plea_for_political_entrepreneurship. Accessed: 28 May 2018.

Wohlgemuth, Michael. "Political Entrepreneurship and Bidding for Political Monopoly." Journal of Evolutionary Economics 10, 273–295. 2000.

Printed by Printforce, the Netherlands